Making Money in

Germany

Business Guide

and Contacts

By

Patrick W. Nee

The Internationalist

www.internationalist.com

Other Titles Featured in the Business Guides Series

MAKING MONEY IN CHINA: Key Business Contacts and Addresses

MAKING MONEY IN CHINA: China Business Guide and Contacts

MAKING MONEY IN CHINA: China Country Guide for Businesses

MAKING MONEY IN RUSSIA: Russia Country Guide for Businesses

MAKING MONEY IN EXPORTING: A Complete Guide to the Business of Exporting

MAKING MONEY IN Brazil: Brazil Business Guide and Contacts

The Internationalist®

International Business, Investment, and Travel

Published by:
The Internationalist Publishing Company
96 Walter Street/Suite 200
Boston MA 02131, USA
Tel: 617-354-7722
www.internationalist.com
PN@internationalist.com

Welcome to the **Internationalist Business Guides** series:

The key to a successful business is knowing the markets. MAKING MONEY IN GERMANY: GERMANY BUSINESS GUIDE AND CONTACTS offers executives, investors, and entrepreneurs the need-to-know information about doing business in Germany.

Written as an in-depth, straightforward reference guide, this book lists key information about the German market, its challenges, and opportunities. It then looks into a dozen of Germany's leading industries, their backgrounds, current situation, and projected course.

Whether you are looking to break into international business or need to update your knowledge on German markets— this comprehensive guide is for you.

The Internationalist

Contents

Chapter 1: Doing Business in Germany

Market Overview

The German economy is the world's fourth largest and, after the expansion of the EU, accounts for more than one-fifth of European Union GDP. Germany is the United States' largest European trading partner and is the sixth largest market for U.S. exports. Germany's "social market" economy largely follows free-market principles, but with a considerable degree of government regulation and generous social welfare programs. Germany is the largest consumer market in the European Union with a population of over 82 million. However, the significance of the German marketplace goes well beyond its borders.

An enormous volume of worldwide trade is conducted in Germany at some of the world's largest trade events, such as MEDICA, Hannover Fair, Automechanika, and the ITB Tourism Show. The volume of trade, number of consumers, and Germany's geographic location at the heart of a 27-member European Union make it a cornerstone around which many U.S. firms seek to build their European and worldwide expansion strategies.

Market Challenges

The German economy has improved markedly in recent years. The economy took a serious hit during the economic crisis, but recovered quickly. Like most other OECD countries GDP declined significantly in 2009 (by 4.7%), but grew by 3.6% in

2010, the highest rate since unification. Following a 3% growth in 2011, the pace of expansion is expected to slow in 2012. Most economic research institutes have lowered their 2012 GDP forecast to 0.6% from 1.0% predicted in October 2011. The labor market remained resilient during the economic crisis and continued to be strong in 2011. In addition to a series of labor and social reforms implemented in recent years, many experts credit the government-funded short-time work program for limiting unemployment.

Other factors, such as moderate wage increases, flexibility in bargaining agreements, numerous company-level alliances to retain jobs, and employers' willingness to accept higher unit labor costs, also contributed to the stability of the German labor market. Job cuts in logistics and manufacturing have been offset by job creation in other sectors, such as services and health care. Also due to a declining workforce, average unemployment dropped to 2.976 million over the course of last year, with an average jobless rate of 7.1% – down from 7.7% in 2010. For 2012, the government expects unemployment to decline to an average of 6.8%.

Although unemployment is still higher in the east of the country than the west (11.3% versus 6.0%), it dropped to the lowest level in 20 years. The number of persons in   employment living in Germany reached an all-time high (about 41.6 million) in November 2011, an increase of 521,000 from a year ago. Germany presents few formal barriers to U.S. trade or investment, although Germany's participation in the EU's Common Agricultural Policy and German restrictions on biotech agricultural products represent barriers for some U.S. goods. Germany has pressed the new EU Commission to reduce regulatory burdens and promote innovation to increase EU member states' competitiveness. The Merkel government has talked about the need for regulatory reform in Germany. In particular, Economics Minister Rainer Bruederle (pro-market Free Democratic Party - FDP) has pushed to reduce bureaucratic costs, since Germany's regulations and bureaucratic procedures can be very complex.

While not directly discriminatory, government regulation by virtue of its complexity may offer a degree of protection to established local suppliers. Safety or environmental standards, not inherently discriminatory but sometimes zealously applied, can complicate access to the market for U.S. products. American companies interested in exporting to Germany should make sure they know which standards apply to their product and obtain timely testing and certification. German standards are especially relevant to U.S. exporters because, as EU-wide standards are developed, they are often based on existing German standards.

Market Opportunities

For U.S. companies, the German market - the largest in the EU - continues to be attractive in numerous sectors and remains an important element of any comprehensive export strategy to Europe. While U.S. investors must reckon with a relatively higher cost of doing business in Germany, they can count on high levels of productivity, a highly skilled labor force, quality engineering, a first-class infrastructure, and a location in the heart of Europe.

Market Entry Strategy

The most successful market entrants are those that offer innovative products featuring high quality and modern styling. Germans are responsive to the innovation and high technology evident in U.S. products, such as computers, computer software, electronic components, health care and medical devices, synthetic materials, and automotive technology. Germany boasts one of the highest Internet access rates in the EU and new products in the multi-media, high-tech and service areas offer great potential as increasing numbers of Germans join the Internet generation. Certain agricultural products also represent good export prospects for U.S. producers. Price is not necessarily the determining factor for the German buyer, given the German market's demand for quality.

The German market is decentralized and diverse, with interests and tastes differing dramatically from one German state to another. Successful market strategies take into account regional differences as part of a strong national market presence. Experienced representation is a major asset to any market strategy, given that the primary competitors for most American products are domestic firms with established presences. U.S. firms can overcome such stiff competition by offering high-quality products, services at competitive prices, and locally based after-sales support. For investors, Germany's relatively high marginal tax rates and complicated tax laws may constitute an obstacle,   although deductions, allowances and write-offs help to move effective tax rates to internationally competitive levels.

Chapter 2: Selling U.S. Products and Services

Using an Agent or Distributor

Companies wishing to use distribution, franchising and agency arrangements need to ensure that the agreements they put into place are in accordance with European Union (EU) and Member State national laws. Council Directive 86/653/EEC establishes certain minimum standards of protection for self-employed commercial agents who sell or purchase goods on behalf of their principals. In essence, the Directive establishes the rights and obligations of the principal and its agents; the agent's remuneration; and the conclusion and termination of an agency contract, including the notice to be given and indemnity or compensation to be paid to the agent. U.S. companies should be particularly aware that the Directive states that parties may not derogate certain requirements. Accordingly, the inclusion of a clause specifying an alternate body of law to be applied in the event of a dispute will likely be ruled invalid by European courts.

The European Commission's Directorate General for Competition enforces legislation concerned with the effects on competition in the internal market of such "vertical agreements." Most U.S. exporters are small- and medium-sized companies (SMEs) and are therefore exempt from the Regulations because their agreements likely would qualify as "agreements of minor importance," meaning they are considered incapable of affecting competition at the EU level but useful for cooperation between SMEs. Generally speaking, companies with fewer than 250 employees and an annual turnover of less than €50 million are considered small- and medium-sized undertakings. The EU has additionally indicated that agreements that affect less than 10 percent of a particular market are generally exempted as well (Commission Notice 2001/C 368/07).

The EU also looks to combat payment delays with Directive 2000/35/EC. This covers all commercial transactions within the EU, whether in the public or private sector, primarily dealing with the consequences of late payment. Transactions with consumers, however, do not fall within the scope of this Directive. In sum, the Directive entitles a seller who does not receive payment for goods/services within 30-60 days of the payment deadline to collect interest (at a rate of 7 percent above the European Central Bank rate) as compensation. The seller may also retain the title to goods until payment is completed and may claim full compensation for all recovery costs. Companies' agents and distributors can take advantage of the European Ombudsman when victim of inefficient management by an EU institution or body. Complaints can be made to the European Ombudsman only by businesses and other bodies with registered offices in the EU. The Ombudsman can act upon these complaints by investigating cases in which EU institutions fail to act in accordance with the law, fail to respect the principles of good administration, or violate fundamental rights.

Data Privacy

The EU's general data protection Directive (95/46/EC) spells out strict rules concerning the processing of personal data. Businesses must tell consumers that they are collecting data, what they intend to use it for, and to whom it will be disclosed.

Data subjects must be given the opportunity to object to the processing of their personal details and to opt- out of having them used for direct marketing purposes. This opt-out should be available at the time of collection and at any point thereafter. This general legislation is supplemented by specific rules set out in the "Directive on the processing of personal data and the protection of privacy in the electronic communications sector" (2002/58/EC). This requires companies to secure the prior consent of consumers before sending them marketing emails. The only exception to this opt-in provision is if the marketer has already obtained the intended recipient's contact details in the context of a previous sale and wishes to send them information on similar products and services.

Transferring Customer Data to Countries outside the EU The EU's general data protection Directive provides for the free flow of personal data within the EU and also for its protection when it leaves the region's borders. Personal data can only be transferred outside the EU if adequate protection is provided for it or if the unambiguous consent of the data subject is secured. The European Commission has decided that a handful of countries have regulatory frameworks in place that guarantee the adequate protection of data transferred to them – the United States is not one of these.

The Department of Commerce and the European Commission negotiated the Safe Harbor agreement to provide U.S. companies with a simple, streamlined means of complying with the adequacy requirement. It allows those U.S. companies that commit to a series of data protection principles (based on the

Directive), and who publicly state that commitment by "self-certifying" on a dedicated website, to continue to receive personal data from the EU. Signing up is voluntary but the rules are binding on those who do. The ultimate means of enforcing Safe Harbor is that failure to fulfill the commitments will be actionable as an unfair and deceptive practice under Section 5 of the FTC Act or under a concurrent Department of Transportation statute for air carriers and ticket agents. While the United States as a whole does not enjoy an adequacy finding, transfers that are covered by the Safe Harbor scheme will. Companies whose activities are not regulated by the FTC or DoT (e.g. banks, credit unions, savings and loan institutions, securities dealers, insurance companies, not-for-profit organizations, meat packing facilities, or telecommunications carriers) are not eligible to sign up to the Safe Harbor.

EU based exporters or U.S. based importers of personal data can also satisfy the adequacy requirement by including data privacy clauses in the contracts they sign with each other. The Data Protection Authority in the EU country from where the data is being exported must approve these contracts. To fast track this procedure the European Commission has approved sets of model clauses for personal data transfers that can be inserted into contracts between data importers and exporters. The most recent were published at the beginning of 2005; work to update these and develop new ones in ongoing. Most transfers using contracts based on these model clauses do not require prior approval.

Companies must bear in mind that the transfer of personal data to third countries is a processing operation that is subject to the general data protection Directive regardless of any Safe Harbor, contractual or consent arrangements. EU countries' Data Protection Authorities (DPAs) and large multinational companies are also developing a third major approach to compliance with EU rules on transfers of personal data to countries outside the EU. This is based on country-by-country approval of "binding corporate rules" (BCRs). Companies that set up BCRs that satisfy European DPAs will be able to use the presumption of conformity that these approvals provide to transfer personal data from the EU to any location in the world – not just the United States. BCRs can be a tool for compliance with privacy rules on a global scale. The process of negotiation and approval of the BCRs is currently lengthy and complex, and has not been attempted by small or medium-sized companies.

Franchising

Germany is a mature franchise market in which local entrepreneurs have developed sophisticated concepts. A high concentration of franchising chains in Germany exists in the service sector (45%), trade (37%), building and handicraft (8%), and gastronomy (10%). Industry sources expect the best prospects to be in the areas of training and educational services; express delivery services (all types); theme bistros/restaurants; office management, accounting and tax services; maintenance, cleaning and sanitation services; advertising; telecommunication products and services; energy saving products and services; retail stores (specialized); home care services; and environmental services. U.S. franchisors must be prepared to adapt to required market norms and standards, invest in market research, test market receptivity through pilot projects, and to adjust their concepts to German business practices and consumer tastes. Restrictions to competition in franchise agreements are generally covered by the Block Exemption on Vertical Restraints of 1999 referred to in the preceding chapter "Distributors."

Direct Marketing

German consumers are accustomed to purchasing via catalog and have become more receptive to shopping on Internet platforms. More than 80% of German enterprises use direct marketing to sell their products and services. The most frequently used formats are email and Internet marketing (65%), telephone marketing (31%), direct mail (24%) and inserts in publications with a response element (18%). Trading companies, manufacturers, and service companies spend more than EUR 30 billion on direct marketing with mailing expenditures clearly in the lead, followed by inserts with response elements, and telephone marketing. Direct marketing agencies currently employ 48,000, a number which is expected to grow over the next years. It is important to know the pitfalls of using direct marketing as a selling tool in Germany. Data protection and privacy laws are stringent, and consumer protection guidelines and competitive advertising are also highly regulated. Companies should consult with a lawyer before raising, storing or processing any sort of data in Germany. Other potential challenges regard the laws pertaining to unfair competition and rebates.

EU Regulations

There is a wide range of EU legislation that impacts the direct marketing sector. Compliance requirements are stiffest for marketing and sales to private consumers. Companies need to focus, in particular, on the clarity and completeness of the information they provide to consumers prior to purchase, and on their approaches to collecting and using customer data. The following gives a brief overview of the most important provisions flowing from EU-wide rules on distance selling and on-line commerce. It is worth noting that the EU is currently overhauling its consumer protection legislation. Companies are advised to consult the information available via the hyper- links, to check the relevant sections of national Country Commercial Guides, and to contact the Commercial Service at the U.S. Mission to the European Union for more specific guidance.

Processing Customer Data

The EU has strict laws governing the protection of personal data, including the use of such data in the context of direct marketing activities. on these rules, please see the privacy section above. Distance Selling Rules Distance and Door-to-Door sales The EU's Directive on distance selling to consumers (97/7/EC) sets out a number of obligations for companies doing business at a distance with consumers. Distance Selling of Financial Services Financial services are the subject of a separate Directive that came into force in June 2002 (2002/65/EC). This piece of legislation amends three prior existing Directives and is designed to ensure that consumers are appropriately protected in respect to financial transactions taking place where the consumer and the provider are not face-to- face.

Direct Marketing Over the Internet

The e-commerce Directive (2000/31/EC) imposes certain specific requirements connected to the direct marketing business. Promotional offers must not mislead customers and the terms that must be met to qualify for them have to be easily accessible and clear. The Directive stipulates that marketing e-mails must be identified as such to the recipient and requires that companies targeting customers on-line must regularly consult national opt-out registers where they exist.

Joint Ventures/Licensing

Dealing with joint ventures ranks among the most difficult jobs under German competition law. In Germany, joint venture legislation falls under the purview of the The law requires that a joint venture must exercise "genuine entrepreneurial" activities. Under German law, this means:

• Organizations which merely carry out auxiliary functions such as purchasing or distribution on behalf of the parents are not considered joint ventures; and

• JVs must have at their disposal sufficient assets and personnel to carry out their activities. The Bundeskartellamt is required to prohibit a merger if it is "expected to create or strengthen a dominant position." Market dominance is defined as an undertaking which either has no competitors or is not exposed to any substantial competition or has a paramount market position in relation to its competitors.

German antitrust law does not, in the absence of a dominant market position, restrict the owner's freedom to use her/his industrial property rights, including the exploitation of a patented innovation.

Selling to the Government

Selling to German government entities is not an easy process. Although there has been a delay in implementing some facets of the EU Utility Directive, German government procurement is formally non-discriminatory and compliant with the GATT Agreement on Government Procurement and the European Community's procurement directives. That said, it is a major challenge to compete head-to-head with major German or other EU suppliers who have established long-term ties with purchasing entities. EU Regulations The EU public procurement market, including EU institutions and Member States, totals around EUR 1,600 billion. This market is regulated by two Directives:

• Directive 2004/18 on Coordination of procedures for the award of public works, services and supplies contracts, and

• Directive 2004/17 on Coordination of procedures of entities operating in the Utilities sector, which covers the following sectors: water, energy, transport and postal services.

Remedies directives cover legal means for companies who face discriminatory public procurement practices. These directives are implemented in the national procurement legislation of the 27 EU Member States. The US and the EU are signatories of the World Trade Organization's (WTO) Government Procurement Agreement (GPA), which grants access to most public supplies and some services and works contracts published by national procuring authorities of the countries that are parties to the Agreement. In practice, this means that U.S.-based companies are eligible to bid on supplies contracts from European public contracting authorities above the agreed thresholds. , please visit the U.S. Commercial Service at the U.S. Mission to the European Union website dedicated to EU public procurement. This site also has a database of all European public procurement tenders that are open to U.S.-based firms by virtue of the Government Procurement Agreement. Access is free of charge.

Distribution and Sales Channels

Distribution channels are varied and similar to the United States. There are certain restrictions, however, concerning multi-level networking systems, i.e., so-called snowball or pyramid distribution systems.

Selling Factors/Techniques

Success in the German market, as elsewhere around the world, requires long-term commitment to market development and sales backup, especially if U.S. companies are to overcome the geographic handicap with respect to European competitors. Germans at times perceive U.S. suppliers as tending to process a U.S. domestic order before taking care of an export sale, or being quick to bypass a local distributor to deal directly with its customer. Some German entrepreneurs with selective experience with U.S. companies are skeptical about their long-term commitment and after-sales support. U.S. firms entering Germany today are generally aware of the factors that make for a successful export relationship and are ready to establish a credible support network. However, U.S. firms should be ready to address any lingering doubts from prospective German clients/partners.

Electronic Commerce

Germany is the European leader in e-commerce and is among the world's most sophisticated markets: Germany, the world's number two exporter after China, is the largest economy in the European Union and the fourth largest in the world. As Europe's most populous nation, Germany also had the largest number of Internet users, 65 million people (80 percent of the population) in 2011. More products are sold online than through traditional mail order. The most popular product categories are music, video, travel, tickets, books and consumer electronics. Price, trust and product diversity play a major role in determining where products are purchased. The most popular online shops are ebay.de, amazon.de, tchibo.de and otto.de. A majority of online retailers is also relying on the traditional offline retail channel. E-commerce revenues will continue to rise in 2012.

Trade Promotion and Advertising

Few countries in the world can match Germany when it comes to leading international trade fairs. Such a reputation should be no surprise given that the trade fair concept was born in Germany during the Middle Ages. Today, Germany hosts a major world-class trade event in virtually every industry sector, attracting buyers from around the world. Trade fairs thrive in Germany because they are true business events where contracts are negotiated and deals are consummated. The U.S. exhibitors at German fairs should be prepared to take full advantage of the business opportunities presented at these events. While U.S. exhibitors and visitors can conclude transactions, all attendees can use major German trade fairs to conduct market research, see what their worldwide competition is doing, and test pricing strategies. Finally, German fairs attract buyers from throughout the world, allowing U.S. exhibitors to conduct business here with buyers from across Europe, Asia, Africa, Latin America, the Middle East, as well as with other U.S. companies. German trade fairs, in general, attract impressive numbers of visitors and exhibitors. This reality confirms the conviction that there is no other venue where an American company can get so much product exposure for its marketing dollar. Trade fairs also provide a U.S. company interested in entering Germany with the opportunity to research its market and the potential of its product properly before making a business decision.

Showcase Europe

Responding to the international nature of German trade shows, the U.S. Commercial Service has a broad-ranging program entitled "Showcase Europe" designed to support U.S. business interests in the expanded European Union. Focused on high priority sectors such as aerospace; energy; medical equipment, including drugs and pharmaceuticals; telecommunications and information technologies; environmental technologies and equipment; and travel and tourism, "Showcase Europe" provides contacts, market information, and commercial guidance for the entire European market region. What makes these programs effective and unique is that they are conducted by trade specialists who regularly work at U.S. embassies and consulates around Europe, but come together at selected trade fairs for the sole purpose of supporting U.S. firms. "Showcase Europe" programs also address trade policy and other business concerns, such as the protection of intellectual property rights and other market impediments to U.S. companies, which are common across Europe.

Advertising

In addition to exhibiting at major German trade fairs, advertising plays a central role in most companies' broad-based marketing programs. Regulation of advertising in Germany is a mix between basic rules and voluntary guidelines developed by the major industry associations. The "Law Against Unfair Competition" established legal rules at the beginning of the 20th Century. Although it has been modified over time, this law continues to be valid today. The law allows suits to be brought if advertising "violates accepted mores." Many advertising practices that are common in the United States, such as offering premiums, are not allowed in Germany. Any planned advertising campaigns should be discussed with a potential business partner or an advertising agency in Germany. There are numerous technical or specialized periodicals that deal with all aspects of technology and doing business in Germany. In addition, Germany has a well-developed array of newspapers and magazines which offer the opportunity to gather information and advertise products and services.

EU Regulations

Laws against misleading advertisements differ widely from Member State to Member State within the EU. To respond to this imperfection in the Internal Market, the Commission adopted a Directive, in force since October 1986, to establish minimum and objective criteria regarding truth in advertising. The Directive was amended in October 1997 to include comparative advertising. Under the Directive, misleading advertising is defined as any "advertising which in any way, including its presentation, deceives or is likely to deceive the persons to whom it is addressed or whom it reaches and which, by reason of its deceptive nature, is likely to affect their economic behavior or which for those reasons, injures or is likely to injure a competitor." Member States can authorize even more extensive protection under their national laws. Comparative advertising, subject to certain conditions, is defined as "advertising which explicitly or by implication identifies a competitor or goods or services by a competitor." Member States can, and in some cases have, restricted misleading or comparative advertising.

Following the adoption of the 1999 Council Directive on the Sale of Consumer Goods and Associated Guarantees, product specifications, as laid down in advertising, are now considered as legally binding on the seller. The EU adopted Directive 2005/29/EC concerning fair business practices in a further attempt to tighten up consumer protection rules. These new rules will outlaw several aggressive or deceptive marketing practices such as pyramid schemes, "liquidation sales" when a shop is not closing down, and artificially high prices as the basis for discounts in addition to other potentially misleading advertising practices. Certain rules on advertising to children are also set out.

Medicine

The advertising of medicinal products for human use is regulated by Council Directive 2001/83/EC. Generally speaking, the advertising of medicinal products is forbidden if market authorization has not yet been granted or if the product in question is a prescription drug. On Nov. 24, 2010, the EU commission passed legislation aiming at providing citizens of EU Member States with understandable, objective, high-quality and non-promotional information about the benefits and the risks of their medicines, while maintaining the ban on direct-to-consumer advertising of prescription medicines and making sure that there is a clear distinction between advertising and non-promotional information.

Food

On July 1, 2007, a regulation on nutrition and health claims entered into force. Regulation 1924/2006 sets EU-wide conditions for the use of nutrition claims such as "low fat" or "high in vitamin C" and health claims such as "helps lower cholesterol." The regulation applies to any food or drink product produced for human consumption that is marketed on the EU market. Only foods that fit a certain nutrient profile (below certain salt, sugar and/or fat levels) will be allowed to carry claims. Nutrition and health claims will only be allowed on food labels if they are included in one of the EU positive lists. Food products carrying claims must comply with the provisions of nutritional labeling directive 90/496/EC. A simplified authorization procedure has been established for health claims based on new scientific data. GAIN Report E48055 describes how application dossiers for authorization of health claims should be prepared and presented.

Food Supplements

Regulation 1925/2006, applicable as of July 1, 2007, harmonizes rules on the addition of vitamins and minerals to foods. The regulation lists the vitamins and minerals that may be added to foods and sets criteria for establishing minimum and maximum levels.

Tobacco

The EU Tobacco Advertising Directive bans tobacco advertising in printed media, radio, and internet as well as the sponsorship of cross-border events or activities. Advertising in cinemas and on billboards or merchandising is allowed though these are banned in many Member States. Tobacco advertising on television has been banned in the EU since the early 1990s and is governed by the "TV Without Frontiers Directive".

Pricing

Germany has become more price-conscious, especially in consumer goods areas. Consequently, price is increasing in importance as a competitive factor, but quality, timely delivery and service remain equally important, especially in the B2B relations.

Sales Service/Customer Support

The German commercial customer expects to be able to pick up the telephone, talk to his or her dealer and have replacement parts or service work immediately available. American exporters should avoid appointing distributors with impossibly large geographic areas, without firm commitments regarding parts inventories or service capabilities, and without agreements on dealer mark-ups.

EU Regulations

Conscious of the discrepancies among Member States in product labeling, language use, legal guarantee, and liability, the redress of which inevitably frustrates consumers in cross-border shopping, the EU institutions have launched a number of initiatives aimed at harmonizing national legislation. Suppliers within and outside the EU should be aware of existing and upcoming legislation affecting sales, service, and customer support.

Product Liability

Under the 1985 Directive on liability for defective products, amended in 1999, the producer is liable for damage caused by a defect in his product. The victim must prove the existence of the defect and a causal link between defect and injury (bodily as well as material). A reduction of liability of the manufacturer is granted in cases of negligence on the part of the victim.

Product Safety

The 1992 General Product Safety Directive introduces a general safety requirement at the EU level to ensure that manufacturers only place safe products on the market. It was revised in 2001 to include an obligation on the producer and distributor to notify the Commission in case of a problem with a given product, provisions for its recall, the creation of a European Product Safety Network, and a ban on exports of products to third countries that are not deemed safe in the EU. Legal Warranties and After-sales Service Under the 1999 Directive on the Sale of Consumer Goods and Associated Guarantees, professional sellers are required to provide a minimum two-year warranty on all consumer goods sold to consumers (natural persons acting for purposes outside their   trade, businesses or professions), as defined by the Directive. The remedies available to consumers in case of non-compliance are:

• repair of the good(s);

• replacement of the good(s);

• a price reduction; or

• rescission of the sales contract.

Protecting Your Intellectual Property

Several general principles are important for effective management of intellectual property rights in the EU and Germany. First, it is important to have an overall strategy to protect IPR. Second, IPR is protected differently in Germany than in the U.S. Third, rights must be registered and enforced in Germany under EU laws. Companies may wish to seek advice from local attorneys or IP consultants. The U.S. Commercial Service can often provide a list of local lawyers upon request.

The EU's legislative framework for copyright protection consists of a series of Directives covering areas such as the legal protection of computer programs, the duration of protection of authors' rights and neighboring rights, and the legal protection of databases. Almost all Member States have fully implemented the rules into national law, and the Commission is now focusing on ensuring that the framework is enforced accurately and consistently across the EU. The on-line copyright Directive (2001/29/EC) addresses the problem of protecting rights holders in the online environment while protecting the interests of users, ISPs and hardware manufacturers. It guarantees authors' exclusive reproduction rights with a single mandatory exception for technical copies (to allow caching), and an exhaustive list of other exceptions that individual Member States can select and include in national legislation. This list is meant to reflect different cultural and legal traditions, and includes private copying "on condition right holders receive fair compensation."

Patents and Trademarks

EU countries have a "first to file" approach to patent applications, as compared to the "first to invent" system currently followed in the United States. This makes early filing a top priority for innovative companies. Unfortunately, it is not yet possible to file for a single EU-wide patent that would be administered and enforced like the Community.

For the moment, the most effective way for a company to secure a patent across a range of EU national markets is to use the services of the European Patent Office (EPO) in Munich. It offers a one-stop-shop that enables rights holders to get a bundle of national patents using a single application. However, these national patents have to be validated, maintained and litigated separately in each Member State.

The EU-wide Community Trademark (CTM) can be obtained via a single language application to the Office of Harmonization in the Internal Market (OHIM) in Alicante, Spain. It lasts ten years and is renewable indefinitely. For companies looking to protect trademarks in three or more EU countries the CTM is a more cost effective option than registering separate national trademarks. On October 1, 2004, the European Commission (EC) acceded to the World Intellectual Property Organization (WIPO) Madrid Protocol. The accession of the EC to the Madrid Protocol established a link between the Madrid Protocol system, administered by WIPO, and the Community Trademark system, administered by OHIM. As of October 1, 2004, Community Trademark applicants and holders are allowed to apply for international protection of their trademarks through the filing of an international application under the Madrid Protocol. Conversely, holders of international registrations under the Madrid Protocol are entitled to apply for protection of their trademarks under the Community Trademark system.

Designs
The EU adopted a Regulation introducing a single Community system for the protection of designs in December 2001. The Regulation provides for two types of design protection, directly applicable in each EU Member State: the registered Community design and the unregistered Community design. Under the registered Community design system, holders of eligible designs

can use an inexpensive procedure to register them with the EU's Office for Harmonization in the Internal Market (OHIM), based in Alicante, Spain. They will then be granted exclusive rights to use the designs anywhere in the EU for up to twenty-five years. Unregistered Community designs that meet the Regulation's requirements are automatically protected for three years from the date of disclosure of the design to the public.

Within the EU, the rights conferred on trademark holders are subject to the principle of "exhaustion." Exhaustion means that once trademark holders have placed their product on the market in one Member State, they lose the right to prevent the resale of that product in another EU country. This has led to an increase in the practice of so called "parallel importing" whereby goods bought in one Member State are sold in another by third parties unaffiliated to the manufacturer. Parallel trade is particularly problematic for the research-based pharmaceutical industry where drug prices vary from country to country due to national price regulation. Community wide exhaustion is spelled out in the Directive on harmonizing trademark laws. In a paper published in 2003, the Commission indicated that it had no plans to propose changes to existing legal provisions.

Chapter 3: Leading Sectors for U.S. Export and Investment

IT Hardware / Software

Due to the ongoing convergence of the IT sectors, it makes sense to follow the industry definitions. The German Association for the IT industry, BitKOM, provides the most reliable data and outlook for this industry and does not necessarily differentiate between the individual segments and does not provide absolute figures for them.

Germany is the fourth largest IT market behind the USA, Japan and China. Germany accounts for approximately one quarter of the EU's total IT market. The German market for IT-Hardware, software and IT services is expected to grow by 4.5 percent in 2012. U.S. computer products are generally viewed as innovative, with superior quality and leading edge technology. Industry-specific and niche products will continue to find good sales opportunities in Germany. U.S. software products are well accepted and the United States is still widely acknowledged as a supplier of innovative and quality software products. The German public sector, along with the banking, insurance, medical and utilities sectors, offers the best opportunities. Despite the fact that the banking sector was badly affected by the financial crisis, financial institutes need to complete or initiate IT projects, due to the strategic role that IT plays in most banking operations.

Best Prospects/Services

Cloud Computing and Mobile Apps have been identified as the main market trends in 2012, followed by IT-Security, Social Media, Virtualization, Business Intelligence, IT- Outsourcing and Business Process Management.

In 2010, Germany's drug market was the fourth largest worldwide after the United States, Japan and China. The German government remains committed to its fiscal austerity program and to further spending cuts by 2014. Market consolidation continues, with Pfizer having integrated Wyeth drug activities in 2010; and Japanese Takeda's purchase of Swiss Nycomed in 2011. Drug prices have been under pressure from de-reimbursement, fixed-level drug pricing and referencing pricing schemes. Between 2010 and 2015, the market is projected to grow annually at 4.8% (prescription drugs at 3.9%), with the fastest growth in the specialized hospital market for new and expensive pharmaceuticals. The statutory health insurance system accounts for about 80% of the market, with tight reimbursement rules, greater use of generics and downward pressure on generic prices due to the rebate system and the full VAT of 19% levied on drug sales. Opportunities also exist for local production, research and acquisition of German drug firms. (Source: BPI-German Pharmaceutical Industry Association)

Sub-Sector Best Prospects
Diagnostic and therapeutic drugs for dementia; auto immune diseases; inflammation; oncology; pain management. Vaccines and cell- and bio-therapeutics; biosimilars; orphan drugs.

Opportunities

Despite sluggish market growth in recent years and increasing competition from generic drug manufacturers as a result of patent expiration, Germany remains an attractive export market to innovative U.S. drugmakers. There has been an increase in sales growth for drugs to treat acute conditions such as cancer, rheumatoid arthritis, and multiple sclerosis as well as for chronic conditions such as cardiovascular diseases, diabetes and preventive medicine. Drugs for rare diseases, so-called Orphan Drugs, with market exclusivity for 10 years in the European Union, should also see good market potential.

Medical Equipment

Germany is Europe's largest market for medical devices and the world's third largest, behind the United States and Japan, accounting for 7% or EUR 21.1 billion in 2011. Although in decline, Germany's population of Germany still accounts for around 20% of the population. Germany counts 2,000 hospitals; 2,000 medical supply stores; 1,200 rehabilitation centers; 21,500 pharmacies; and 150,000 doctors' offices. At over 11% of GDP in 2010, healthcare expenditures continue to remain at high levels but are constrained by health reforms and cost-cutting measures with continued downward pressure on prices. Government funding of hospital projects has remained static; major areas of opportunity are seen for private hospitals and clinics, which have a 20% market share. Demand will mainly be driven by demographics and a substantial increase in the number of patients and by the need for more efficient procedures.

The German medical market expects a sales growth of approximately 6% this year, with continued upwards trends predicted for next year as well. The medical technology sector continues to be strong on innovation and growth and will provide excellent potential for U.S. suppliers of innovative and price-competitive products. U.S. medical device exporters to Germany continue to hold a 27-30% import market share, depending on product. (Sources: Spectaris Trade Association; BVMED Trade Association; Eucomed; Statista)

U.S. medical device exporters will find good market potential for the following products: high quality advanced diagnostic and therapeutic equipment; innovative technologies and minimally invasive equipment, such as laser-optics in vascular surgery, urology, gastrology, dermatology, and neuro-surgery, new diagnostic and imaging devices, as well as specialized wound care and easy-to-use home care products. The trend is toward demand for miniaturized electro-medical equipment and nano-technology products. Preventive diagnostics and medical products, innovative orthopedic and physiotherapy devices, and biomaterial, cardiovascular and endoscopy products will also find good markets in Germany. Natural orifice surgery, novel imaging technologies, e- health and e-care, mobile medical products are also in demand in Germany. Keywords are: computerization-electronic diagnosis; therapy planning and survey; molecularization-biotechnology, cell and tissue engineering, personalized medicine; miniaturization-microsystems technologies, nanotechnology and optical technologies.

The "Medical Technology Action Plan" pools the Federal Ministry of Education and Research's varied funding activities and programs under three main topics: Medical technology in rehabilitation and care (intelligent implants); Molecular imaging; Medical technology for regenerative medicine. Incentives are provided as R&D project grants/cash incentives with a maximum 50% of eligible project costs. The European Union is subsidizing transnational R&D through its 7th Research Framework Program. A budget of 6.1 billion Euros for the period 2007 to 2013 has been earmarked for health research.

Industrial Chemicals

In 2009, the financial crisis impacted the German chemical market. It improved quickly throughout 2010, reaching full recovery by the end of 2011. In 2011, local chemical production increased by 5% over 2010, German chemical exports grew by approximately 6% to USD 211 billion, pharmaceutical ingredients were particularly high in demand. Insiders anticipate a moderate growth rate for chemical imports from abroad, including imports from the United States, over the next two years. With regard to annual sales in the overall German chemical market, insiders forecast a new sales record for 2011. For the first time in history, German chemical sales are expected to exceed EUR 180 billion or USD 243 billion. Nevertheless, the difficult financial situation in some EU member states led to more cautious purchasing patterns during the second half of 2011; German firms used up their chemical stocks and ordered less. If the German economy continues its upward trend, good growth in the German chemicals market over the next few years can be expected. Growth rates of approximately 5% annually are possible. (Source: German Chemical Association (VCI)) Germany offers good business opportunities across all chemical sub-sectors to U.S. companies manufacturing innovative chemicals. "Green" products are of particular interest: Chemicals based on natural ingredients, i.e., plastics based on PLA, corn, soy beans, algae etc., or substances processed with natural substances such as detergents produced by enzymes. Also in demand are renewable chemicals; innovative coatings and adhesives; photovoltaic chemicals, i.e., additives for plastics that enhance electrical conductivity; high performance solvents; reactive substances for UV sensitive materials, i.e., photo initiators; fuel cell chemicals; innovative APIs or other substances new to the world chemical market. U.S. companies can often supply several EU markets by signing up with one single German distributor.

Management Consulting Services

Germany is the largest consulting market in Europe, followed by the UK. In 2011, around 91,000 management consultants worked in about 14,100 consulting firms. The segment experienced a booming year in 2011 with revenues increasing by 9.5 percent. Demand was especially strong in the automotive (up 19 percent) and consumer goods (up 14.3 percent) industries. The two largest consulting fields are strategic and organizational/process consulting. Consulting firms throughout Germany tend to be located in various regional centers, rather than in one city serving as a national center.

Best Products/Services

A continued growth of 7 percent is expected in 2012. More than half of the demand for consulting services comes from clients in both the manufacturing and financial services industries. A demand increase is expected in the consumer goods, machinery and automotive sectors in 2012. Changing business models will be a priority for projects with financial service providers and utility companies. Projects related to growth, innovation, business development, marketing and sales are expected to grow. Clients demand assurance for concrete added value of consulting projects.

Automotive Parts

For Germany, the automotive industry is still the most important manufacturing industry sector, accounting for roughly 20% of Germany's total industrial sales and to a little over 719,000 employees. In 2011, sales reached about EUR 474 billion (+10.7%). The automotive parts and accessories sector accounted for EUR 93.3 billion (+12.3%). The German automotive industry has recovered quickly from the recent economic crisis due to its strong commitment to innovation and continuous investments in R&D. Many of the industry's technological advances take place on the supplier side. In 2010, investments in R&D were around EUR 27 billion, which accounts for more than one third of total R&D-spending in Germany. The automotive industry is expecting future growth especially in foreign markets in North and South America as well as Asia (China and India). German OEMs produced a total of roughly 12.7 million vehicles in 2010 (11.6 million passenger cars), whereas 5.9 million were produced in Germany (5.5 million passenger cars).

Best Products/Services

E-mobility; (integrated) mobility services and concepts; emission control/reduction technologies; climate control systems; engine electronics; automotive semiconductors, LED lighting; Software, IT, and communication technology (smart driving assistance and entertainment); alternative drives (electric/hybrid/fuel cell technology etc.) as well as components; Clean Diesel technologies; light weight materials such as carbon fiber parts, e.g. (CFRP) etc.; "downsizing" technologies; technologies to enhance the range extension of EVs.

Telecommunications Equipment and Services

ICT companies' outlook in general is optimistic. Fixed line data and voice services and demand for mobile voice services show moderate growth, mobile data services has been declining for some time, Broadband will remain the key application with more than 7 million connections and a penetration rate of 8 percent. DSL will continue to represent the overwhelming majority of broadband connections, with Deutsche Telekom (DTAG) providing more than 83% of all broadband connections. Demand for mobile phones is beginning to decline due to market saturation. Equipment suppliers hope that they can benefit from planned government investment (EUR 130 million) in infrastructure and especially schools. (Source: RegTP, EITO, Bitkom)

Best Products/Services

Broadband equipment and services, W-Lan equipment and services.

Opportunities

Broadband technologies (DSL and TV cable) will offer considerable opportunities for suppliers of technology and services.

Sporting Goods The German sporting goods market is expected to grow annually by at least 0.5% over the next two years. The German sporting goods industry is characterized by mostly medium-sized enterprises with nearly 120,000 employees. The wide ranging production lines (about 10,000 items) split into four product groups with corresponding percentages of the total production: Sports & Leisure Equipment (37.9%), Sports Apparel/Sports Shoes (27.7%), Camping & Trekking Goods/Tents etc. (27.3%), Garden & Camping Furniture (7.1%). In 2010, winter sports equipment and accessories experienced annual sales increases of 20%. The same applied to the outdoor market in 2010, while fitness equipment achieved another 5% increase in sales compared to 2009, and running, Nordic walking and racket sports 3%, respectively. Over the last decade, Germany maintained the position of the 3rd largest importer within the EU. Major competitors in the German market include China (approx. 50% import market share), Italy (approx. 9%), Poland (approx. 8%), the Netherlands and France (both approx. 4%), and the Czech Republic (approx. 3%). About 84% of all exports are purchased by EU member states. The U.S. ranks second after Switzerland among the most important non-EU buying countries, followed by Russia, Japan, Turkey and, to an increasing degree, China.

Despite economic uncertainties, the German sporting goods market is expected to grow moderately over the next few years, fueled largely by the increasing numbers of elderly consumers taking up a more active lifestyle. Germany already has the largest proportion (25 million) of the 50+ age group – the so-called "Best Agers" – within the EU, which is expected to grow more rapidly than elsewhere. Sports activities remain a mega trend in Germany, thus offering excellent opportunities for U.S. sports products manufacturers. Beside winter sports, the demand for the all-season boom segment of outdoor sports, as well as individual and team sports activities (e.g. running, golf, riding, swimming, soccer), are expected to further increase. (Sources: German Sporting Goods Manufacturers Association; German Association of Sporting Goods Retailers; Individual Research)

Sub-Sector Best Prospects

Fitness equipment for physical exercise, gymnastics, or track and field; footwear (all sports); golf equipment; inflatable balls for soccer, basketball, field hockey, handball; in- line skates; outdoor goods for hiking, climbing, trekking, and Nordic walking activities; roller blades; snowboards.

Travel & Tourism

In 2012, German travel abroad is expected to grow by 2 %, according to Reisestudie 2012 conducted by Commerzbank. In a recent survey, 45 % of German respondents stated they would travel at least once for more than 5 days in 2012. Germany ranks number one in travel expenditure worldwide and third in arrivals to the United States from overseas (Canada and Mexico not included). The United States are the most popular long-haul destination for German travelers. Travel to the United States increased by 6 % in 2011 and is expected to grow by an overall

36 % from 2010 to 2016. The most popular U.S. states for German travelers are New York, California and Florida, with New York City being the most popular city. In several other states, German travelers are the top overseas visitors. German travelers are especially interested in specialized offers tailored to fit their individual preferences. There is a strong preference for all-inclusive packages and vacations. The average length of stay for German tourists in the United States is considerably longer than for other overseas visitors. Several hundred non-stop flights take off from Germany to the United States each week. In short, German demand for travel will slightly grow in 2012. Especially domestic tourism has become a trend. However, the United States continues to be the favorite long-haul destination. The overall economic situation and uncertainty may impact German travel this year.

Best Products/Services City packages including wellness and a unique travel experience; a focus on value for money; all-inclusive packages; nature- hiking and camping holidays; Native American inventory packaged with local attractions and service providers, which should be activity- based rather than language dependent; incentives for small groups.

Renewable Energies

As prices for conventional fuels continue to increase and prices for renewable energy steadily decrease, the renewable energy sector is expected to continue growing. Electricity generation from renewable energies is substantially based on the German Renewable Energy Sources Act (Erneuerbare-Energien-Gesetz, EEG), which is in accordance with European policy (Directive

2001/77/EC). The share of renewable energy sources in the total energy consumption (heat, electricity and fuels) is expected to reach at roughly 30% by 2020.

Best Products/Services

Application areas:

In 2020, renewable energy resources are expected to generate 28% of the entire energy. This figure can be broken down into 47% of the entire electricity, 25% of all heating energy, and 22 % of all fuels used for transportation purposes (ships, automobiles, trucks, and electricity for electric vehicles and trains).

Wind Energy: Of all renewable energy sources, wind energy will remain the most significant. Until 2020, 20%, or 115 TWh/aelec., of the entire electric consumption in Germany is expected to be met by wind energy. A major share of the increased yield will come from on shore repowering. The highest growth rates will be realized in the off shore segment.

Bio Energy: In 2020, bio energy will account for 54 TWh/aelec. or 9.1% of all electricity, 150 TWh/athermal or 13% of heating energy, and 111 TWh/a or 21% of all fuels. The major share will come from biogas, followed by solid biomass (mainly wood and plants), liquid biomass (plant oils), and sewage and landfill gas. Photovoltaic (PV) and Solar Thermal Energy Only about 6% of the entire suitable roofs (not considering free standing installations) are being used for solar energy purposes at present in Germany. In 2020, 39.5 GW/p of installed cells will generate 40 TWh/aelec.. PV will then generate around 7% of the electricity used in Germany. Solar thermal heating energy is expected to increase to an annual yield of 30TWh/a/thermal in 2020.

Hydro Power: Most hydro power plants operating in Germany were built before the 1960s and the majority is in the 5-10 MW class. Experts state that the present 20 TWh/aelec. that are presently generated can be increased (mainly by repowering existing plants) to over 31 TWh/aelec. by 2020 and then account for 5.4% of the electric power generation in Germany. In addition to repowering, major investment is also expected for environmental protection measures for hydro power plant surrounding waterways (fish steps, re-naturalization of riverbeds, and optimization of river flow).

Geothermal Energy Industrial, deep geothermal energy: At present, total installed electrical power equals to 7.3 MW generating 19 GWh and 6,300 GWhthermal per year. It is expected that this energy form will reach as much as 6000 MW installed capacity generating 38 TWhelec. and 14,400 GWhthermal by 2020. Surface geothermal energy: In 2011 over 60,000 heat pumps were installed, mostly in private residences bringing the total number of heat pumps to over 350,000 units. More than half use water-to-water or brine-to-water technology for which vertical drilling or horizontal netting is required. A little less than half use air-to-air heat pump technology, which is expected to carry the highest growth potential.

Scientific and Laboratory Instrumentation
After a decline in 2009 due to the economic and financial crisis, the market for laboratory and scientific instruments picked up

again by 7% in 2010 and has continued to grow at that pace. The German market for Laboratory and Scientific Instruments is very competitive and German companies are famous for innovation, customer-specific solutions, special niche products as well as for their flexibility and customer service. About 9% of the overall sales of the 330 German manufacturers active in that industry (many of which are SMEs) are invested into research and development. Despite the competitiveness of local suppliers, the German market is very open to imports. Main import sources in 2010 were the U.S., Japan and Switzerland. The main end users are the industry, the public sector, pharmaceutical and chemical companies, the environmental sector, chemical and medical laboratories, biotechnology and nutraceutical firms as well as entities for research and development. Hence, the market for the S&LI sector heavily depends on the development in these industry segments.

Sub-Sector Best Prospects

Laboratory automation and information systems (LIMS), as well as the broad spectrum of chromatographic technologies; other trends within the S&LI industry are automation, process analysis, and miniaturization. Laser and opto-electronic instrumentation (primarily for medical applications – applications for the automotive and semiconductor industries are presently declining). Within the laser and optoelectronics field, laser products for the solar industry will play an important role in the future.

Agricultural Sectors

Best Prospects for Agricultural Products

1. Tree Nuts

The category of tree nuts includes almonds, walnuts, pistachios, pecans, hazelnuts and cashew nuts. Germany does not produce significant quantities of these products, therefore, supply comes primarily from imports. A number of U.S. agricultural associations actively promote their products in Germany, including the Almond Board of California, California Pistachio Commission and the California Walnut Commission. The leading competitor for the United States in the German tree nut market is Turkey. In 2010, U.S. tree nut exports to Germany were valued at $494 million out of a total import value of $1.4 billion.

2. Fishery Products

Fish and fishery products enjoy growing popularity in Germany. The two most important fishery products the U.S. exports to Germany by volume are frozen fillets of Alaska pollock and hake. In 2010, U.S. total exports of fishery products to Germany were valued at $215 million, out of a total import value of $4.5 billion. China and Peru are the main U.S. competitors for Alaska pollock and hake exports, respectively.

3. Wine

Germany is the world's largest importer of wine. In 2011, German wine imports were valued at more than $3 billion. Italy, France and Spain are the leading suppliers of wine to Germany with a combined import market share of 75%. U.S. wines, together with other "new-world" wines, have developed an increasingly good reputation for quality in the German market.

In 2011, the value of Germany's imports of U.S. wines totaled approximately $100 million.

4. Pet Food

Germany is one of the leading countries for pet ownership in the world. Germans are willing to pay a premium to properly feed their pets and interest in specialty health pet food products is growing rapidly. The majority of pet foods are produced domestically and the EU requires pet foods to be derived from meat that is fit for human consumption. The value of U.S. pet food exports to Germany totaled $2 million in 2010, out of a total import value of $807 million. Despite the bureaucratic obstacles, opportunities for exporting pet food products to Germany are available given the considerable size of the market.

Chapter 4: Trade Regulations and Standards

Import Tariffs

U.S. exporters seeking to enter the German market can obtain useful information from the Office of European Union and Regional Affairs at the U.S. Department of Commerce. When provided with a product's Schedule B Number, the Office for EU and Regional Affairs supplies tariff information for American products exported to Germany.

Import Turnover Tax

All industrial imports into Germany are subject to an "Import Turnover Tax" of 19%, which is charged on the duty-paid value of the import article plus the customs duty, which varies by item. (Exemptions: certain agricultural and a few other products, which are taxed 7% ad valorem.) The Import Turnover Tax is designed to place the same tax burden on imported goods as goods produced domestically, on which is levied a 19% "Value-added Tax" (VAT). The German customs authorities collect both customs duty and Import Turnover Tax. It is important, however, to collect and present all invoices as originals in order to deduct any VAT charges from one's own tax liability or to get reimbursed by the German Ministry of Finance, if eligible.

Trade Barriers

Germany's regulations and bureaucratic procedures can be a difficult hurdle for companies wishing to enter the market and require close attention by U.S. exporters. Complex safety standards, not normally discriminatory but sometimes zealously applied, complicate access to the market for many U.S. products. U.S. suppliers are well advised to do their homework thoroughly and make sure they know precisely which standards apply to their product and that they obtain timely testing and certification.

Import Requirements and Documentation

The Integrated Tariff of the Community, referred to as TARIC (Tarif Intégré de la Communauté), is designed to show various rules applying to specific products being imported into the customs territory of the EU or, in some cases, when exported from it. To determine if a license is required for a particular product, check the TARIC. The TARIC can be searched by country of origin, Harmonized System (HS) Code, and product description on the interactive website of the Directorate-General for Taxation and the Customs Union. Many EU Member States maintain their own list of goods subject to import licensing. For example, Germany's "Import List" (Einfuhrliste) includes goods for which licenses are required, their code numbers, any applicable restrictions, and the agency that will issue the relevant license. The Import List also indicates whether the license is required under German or EU law. Imported goods must be accompanied by a customs declaration, which has to be submitted in writing, and an invoice in duplicate. Normally the German importer files this declaration. The commercial invoice must show the country of purchase and the country of origin of the goods. The invoice should contain:

• Name (company) and address of seller and buyer
• Place and date of issue
• Number, kind of packages

- Precise description of articles
- Volume or quantity in normal commercial units
- Invoice price (in invoice currency)
- Terms of delivery and
- Payment

In addition, a certificate of origin may be required in some cases. Import duties and taxes are subject to change and companies are well advised to verify the correct tariff level shortly before carrying out any export transaction.

The summary declaration is to be lodged by:
- the person who brought the goods into the customs territory of the Community or by any person who assumes responsibility for carriage of the goods following such entry; or
- the person in whose name the person referred to above acted. Non-EU goods presented to customs must be assigned a customs-approved treatment or use authorized for such non-Community goods.

Where goods are covered by a summary declaration, the formalities for them to be assigned a customs-approved treatment or use must be carried out:
- 45 days from the date on which the summary declaration is lodged in the case of goods carried by sea;
- 20 days from the date on which the summary declaration is lodged in the case of goods carried other than by sea.

Where circumstances so warrant, the customs authorities may set a shorter period or authorize an extension of the period. The

Modernized Customs Code (MCC) of the European Union entered into force on 24 June 2008. The MCC replaced Regulation 2913/92 and simplifies various procedures such as introducing a paperless environment, centralized clearance, and more.

U.S. Export Controls

The Wassenaar Arrangement on Export Controls for Conventional Arms and Dual-Use Goods and Technologies is one of four multilateral export control regimes in which the United States and Germany participate. The Arrangement's purpose is to contribute to regional and international security and stability by promoting transparency and greater responsibility in transfers of conventional arms and dual-use (i.e., those having both civil and military uses) goods and technologies to prevent destabilizing accumulations of those items. The Wassenaar Arrangement establishes lists of items for which member countries are to apply export controls. Member governments implement these controls to ensure transfers of the controlled items do not contribute to the development or enhancement of military capabilities that undermine the goals of the Arrangement and are not diverted to support such capabilities. In addition, the Wassenaar Arrangement imposes some reporting requirements on its member governments.

The U.S. Government controls all items for export that are controlled multilaterally by the Wassenaar Arrangement. In general, export controls for dual-use goods and technologies controlled in the Wassenaar Arrangement are administered by the U.S. Department of Commerce and controlled for National

Security reasons on the Commerce Control List. The U.S. Department of State administers export controls on conventional arms.

Temporary Entry

For temporary entry it is usually advisable to purchase an ATA Carnet, which allows for the temporary, duty-free entry of goods into over 50 countries, and is issued by the United States Council for International Business by appointment of the U.S. Customs.

Labeling and Marking Requirements

The European Union does not generally legislate packaging and labeling requirements, but does so for what it sees as specific high-risk products. In the absence of any EU- wide rules, the exporter has to consult national regulations or inquire about voluntary agreements among forwarders that affect packaging and labeling of containers, outside packaging, etc. Importers or freight forwarders should be able to advise U.S. exporters on shipping documents and outer packaging/labeling. European Union customs legislation only regulates administrative procedures, such as type of certificate and the mention of rule of origin on the customs forms and shipping documents. Product-specific packaging and labeling requirements applicable throughout the EU apply to food, medicines, chemicals, pharmaceuticals and other items EU authorities regard as high-risk. The stated purpose of harmonizing such legislation throughout the EU is to minimize the risk for consumers (the end user). The CE mark is mandatory in the EU countries for any electrical apparatus and often more than one CE mark law may apply.

Eco-Label

Since its inception ten years ago, many companies have recognized the benefits of adopting the EU Eco-Label scheme. There are currently 135 companies licensed under the regime, and it has been awarded to 21 product groups. The products range from paints, detergents, and refrigerators to tourist accommodation. The number is growing and it is the only voluntary scheme that covers products moving across borders within the EU. It sets ecological criteria for a range of products and services in a transparent way so that the consumer can make a more informed choice in order to support sustainable consumption patterns. The EU Eco-Label program takes the lifecycle (from cradle to grave) of a product into account, e.g., the materials, health implications, and waste factors that may have an impact on the environment. The "Blue Angel" is a voluntary environmental labeling program created in 1978. It is the oldest environment-related label in the world. The mark is awarded to products and services, which are beneficial to the environment. High standards of occupational health and safety, ergonomics, economical use of raw materials, service life and disposal are also factors covered under this "seal of approval."

According to the German Ministry for Environmental Affairs, the Blue Angel offers companies the opportunity to document their environmental competence in a simple and inexpensive way, thereby enhancing their market image. About 3,700 products and services have been awarded the label, including, recently, mobile phones and marine transport. An overview of EU mandatory and voluntary labeling and marking requirements has been compiled in a market research report.

Agricultural Products

General Veterinary Requirements: In April 1997, the U.S. and the EU reached an equivalency agreement on an overall framework for recognizing each other's veterinary inspection systems. The veterinary equivalency agreement covers more than USD 1.5 billion in U.S. animal product exports to the EU and an equal value of EU exports to the United States. The agreement preserved most pre-existing trade in products, such as pet food, dairy, and egg products. All beef and pork exported to Germany for human consumption must come from slaughterhouses, cutting plants, and cold stores approved for export to the EU. Since 1989, the EU has prohibited imports of beef from cattle treated with growth hormones. Soon after this ban went into effect, an agreement was reached between the United States and the EU that allows American producers of beef from animals not treated with hormones to export to the EU under certain conditions.

Beef

The EU beef market is insulated from the world market by high import duties but still 5 % of its supply is imported. Import opportunities do exist, however, for selected products that are covered by fixed, relatively low tariffs or special quota. Most notably, the EU grants market access through a quota for annual imports of up to 11,500 MT of high-quality beef (HQB) from the United States and Canada. Beef entering the EU under the HBQ tariff-rate quota are subject to a 20 percent duty. In addition, starting in 2009, an autonomous tariff quota for high quality beef at zero percent duty was established on August 1, 2009, for a period of three years for up to 20,000 MT per July/June marketing year. With mutual agreement, the quota is expected to be expanded to 48,200 MT after this period, on August 1 2012. Pork: Selected market opportunities exist for imports of pork. Market access within the EU has improved through the creation of a tariff-rate quota (TRQ) totaling 67,869 MT. The TRQ includes a 40,265 MT allocation for tenderloins, boneless loins and boneless hams. In addition, a 4,722 MT TRQ is reserved for boneless loins and boneless hams from the United States.

Poultry

Unfortunately, U.S. and EU negotiators have not been able to reach agreement on a number of important points during the veterinary equivalency negotiations, particularly in the poultry sector. The most contentious issue is the use of pathogen reduction treatments in U.S. poultry processing. Most forms of anti-microbial treatments are prohibited in the EU. The EU's ban on anti-microbial treatments effectively blocks U.S. poultry exports to the EU, which were estimated at USD 50 million in 1996.

Dairy Products

The veterinary agreement allows for U.S. dairy products export to Germany and the EU from approved establishments under a fixed tariff. Pet food: U.S. pet food exports to the EU must comply with EU regulation 1774/2002. This regulation, implemented in 2004, requires that animal by-products used in the production of feeds and pet food be derived from the carcasses of animals declared fit for human consumption following veterinary inspection. Provisions include a ban on intra-species recycling, fallen stock and restrictions on yellow grease. Certain categories of pet food have to be denatured with specified substances. Pet food plants have to be dedicated to the production of product fit for human consumption.

Plant Health

As part of the Single Market exercise, plant health regulations in the 27 European Union Member States have been harmonized. The regulations went into effect on June 1, 1993, for the 15 members then in the EU and in 2004 for the new accession countries. The EU has been successful in reducing the number of phytosanitary restrictions and new marketing opportunities have been created for U.S. horticultural exports. Phytosanitary certificates are required for many imported fresh products. With respect to the use of solid wooden packing materials (SWPM), it is important to note that the EU requires that all SWPM be either heat treated or fumigated beginning July 1, 2009. In addition to these treatment requirements, the material has to be free of bark. EU scientists fear that improperly treated SWPM is at risk for re-infestation. International plant protection standards as agreed upon by the United States do not require the absence of bark. Exporters should carefully follow the status of EU import requirements to avoid problems at the EU port of entry.

Horticultural Products

Germany is an important market for United States horticultural products. Principal products include almonds, walnuts, pistachios, prunes, raisins, citrus, and pears. Horticultural products entering Germany face a number of import restrictions. In addition to considerable tariffs that vary by product, imports of selected produce (tomatoes, cucumber, artichokes, zucchini squash, citrus, table grapes, apples, pears, apricots, cherries, peaches, nectarines and plums) are subject to an entry price system. Under such a system, imports that have a price at or above the respective entry price are assessed only the appropriate ad valorem duty. Imports, which have a price below, but within a certain range of the entry price, are assessed the ad valorem duty plus a specific duty that is the difference between the import price and the entry price. "Within a certain range" generally means within eight percent of the entry price. Imports having a price more than 8% below the entry price are assessed the ad valorem duty plus a very large specific duty (known as the tariff equivalent) which generally takes the cost of the product (import price plus duties) far above the entry price.

Organic Products

Germany is the largest market for organic products in the EU with an annual turnover of more than 6 billion Euro (approx. USD 8 billion) in 2010. Until 2008 the German organic market had been growing at near double digital rates annually. In 2009, this growth leveled off as demand for organic products in conventional food stores decreased by several percentage points. Sales through specialized organic food stores are still increasing. The share of organic production in German agriculture is estimated to be about six percent of the total agricultural area and eight percent of the farms.

The European Union and the United States announced February 15, 2012, that beginning June 1, 2012, organic products certified in Europe or in the United States may be sold as organic in either region. This partnership between the two largest organic-producers in the world will reduce duplicative requirements and lower certification costs for the trade in organic products. Growing demand in the EU, supported by the arrangement, is creating new export opportunities for U.S. companies in the following market segments: tree nuts, fresh fruit, specialty grains, dried fruit, vegetables, and processed food products.

Consumer-Ready Products

Imports of consumer-ready food products into Germany face many market access restrictions and very strict food laws. In addition to bound import duties, the EU has established a complex system of border protection measures for food products. Depending on the world market situation for basic agricultural commodities, such as dairy products, sugar and cereals the EU mechanism of flexible tariffs may require variable import duties to protect European consumer-ready food products from imports made with lower-price inputs. Therefore, at many times processed products entering the EU are subject to additional import charges based on the percentage of sugar, milk fat, milk protein, and starch contained in the product. These additional import charges have made many imported processed food products non- competitive in the EU market.

Packaging Disposal

With the tremendous increase in waste and disposal problems, Germany has established legislation that contains certain rules for the disposal of packaging materials. In response to this legislation, a cooperative effort for the collection and recycling of packaging materials was initiated. The organization involved is called the "Duales System Deutschland" and it administers the use of the "Green Dot," a recycling symbol that is found on the packaging material of virtually all products sold in Germany. While packaging materials for products sold in Germany are not legally required to carry the Green Dot, it is almost impossible to market a product in Germany without it. Typically, the importer pays a license fee to the user of the Green Dot, depending on the type and amount of packaging, and provides the exporter with the information necessary.

In 2003, German retailers began requesting a deposit for disposable or "one-way" drink packages, i.e., soft drink or beer cans. Since the requested deposit is about three times as high as that requested for returnable beer bottles, it could disadvantage imported drinks. U.S. Agricultural Commodity Associations Active in Germany A number of U.S. agricultural commodity and other trade associations conduct market development programs in Germany. In some cases, these associations maintain field offices in Germany, while others may have a trade representative or public relations company representing their interests. Others may cover Germany from elsewhere in Europe or from offices in the United States. The USDA-operated Market Access Program (MAP) and Foreign Market Development program (FMD) provides a portion of the funding for the market development programs of these associations.

Customs Regulations

Products tested and certified in the United States to American standards are likely to have to be retested and re-certified to EU requirements as a result of the EU's different approach to the protection of the health and safety of consumers and the environment. Where products are not regulated by specific EU technical legislation, they are always subject to the EU's General Product Safety Directive as well as to possible additional national requirements. European Union standards created under the New Approach are harmonized across the 27 EU Member States and European Economic Area countries to allow for the free flow of goods. A feature of the New Approach is CE marking. While harmonization of EU legislation can facilitate access to the EU Single Market, manufacturers should be aware that regulations and technical standards might also function as barriers to trade if U.S. standards are different from those of the European Union.

Most manufacturers believe the EU's attempt to harmonize the various product safety requirements and related standards for industrial products of its member states has generally helped open member state markets. It did not, however, eliminate entirely voluntary national requirements, a fact which complicates the issue. Theoretically, during a transition period, national requirements must be met. (After the transition period, the EU "CE" mark supersedes all other compliance certificates, provided the products in question are covered by an EU directive.) The EU's efforts to harmonize standards through the "New Approach" certification-facilitating directives (and separately developed European standards) are incomplete as far as sectors covered. In some cases, U.S. firms (for example, in the automotive or pharmaceutical sectors) will have to worry about complying with the specific requirements of all applicable "Old Approach" product-specific EU technical legislation. This is doubly important because, to the extent EU-wide standards are developed, there is a high probability that the existing German standard will form the basis for the eventual European standard. In many cases, Germany will also be the first member country to implement EU-wide standards.

The implementation of electromagnetic compatibility standards (EMC), despite a five-year phase-in period, surprised many affected companies - not only foreign, but also German. German buyers may require additional performance or quality marks, which are not necessarily legally required, but which greatly enhance a product's chances of being marketed. Both EU requirements and the standards for a German quality or performance mark will, in many cases, require modifications for an imported product. Even if the product does not require modification, it may still need testing and certification before it can be marketed.

Two non-mandatory marks which may still be critical to successfully marketing products in Germany are the "geprüfte Sicherheit" (GS) mark, for mechanical products, and the "Verband Deutscher Elektrotechniker" (VDE) mark for electrical components. Neither the "GS" nor the "VDE" mark are mandatory for most products sold in Germany except for products for use in certain work place applications, where these marks are required to meet insurance requirements. However, many German consumers look for these marks as an additional sign of quality, similar to the UL mark in the U.S., regardless of legal requirement.

Standards Organizations

Standards setting is a process based on consensus initiated by industry or mandated by the European Commission and carried out by independent standards bodies, acting at the national, European or international level. There is strong encouragement for non- governmental organizations, such as environmental and consumer groups, to actively participate in European standardization. Many standards in the EU are adopted from international standards bodies such as the International Standards Organization (ISO). Standards are created or modified by experts in Technical Committees or Working Groups. The members of CEN and CENELEC are the national standards bodies of the Member States, which have "mirror committees" that monitor and participate in ongoing European standardization.

The German organization that compiles standards is the Deutscher Industrie Normenausschuss – DIN. The DIN also compiles the standards that lay down the requirements for a "GS" mark. Since 1975, DIN has been recognized by the German government as the national standards body and represents Germany's interests at the international and EU levels. DIN offers a forum in which interested parties meet in order to discuss and define their specific standardization requirements and to record the results as German Standards. In DIN, standard work is carried out by some 26,000 external experts, serving as voluntary delegates in more than 4,000 committees. Draft standards are published for public comment, and all comments are reviewed before final publication of the standard. Published standards are reviewed for continuing relevance at least every five years.

According to DIN, standards are designed to promote rationalization, quality assurance, safety, and environmental protection, as well as improving communication between industry, technology, science, government, and the public domain. The input of external experts into standardization is organized through standards committees and working groups. Each standards committee is responsible for a distinct area of activity and coordinates the corresponding standardization work at the EU and international levels. As a rule, the standards committee in DIN includes a number of technical sub-committees. There are currently 76 standards committees that maintain their own websites. Service Member countries of the World Trade Organization (WTO) are required under the Agreement on Technical Barriers to Trade (TBT Agreement) to report to the WTO all proposed technical regulations that could affect trade with other Member countries. Notify U.S. is a free, web-based e-mail subscription service that offers an opportunity to review and comment on proposed foreign technical regulations that can affect your access to international markets.

Conformity Assessment

Conformity Assessment is a mandatory step for the manufacturer in the process of complying with specific EU legislation. The purpose of conformity assessment is to ensure consistency of compliance during all stages of the production process to facilitate acceptance of the final product. EU product legislation gives manufacturers some choice with regard to conformity assessment, depending on the level of risk involved in the use of their product. These range from self-certification, type examination and production quality control system, to full quality assurance system. You can find conformity assessment bodies in individual Member State country in this list by the European Commission. Accreditation of conformity assessment bodies Conformity assessment bodies evaluate the competence of German entities to carry out tests and certifications in accordance with third country law. Following a successful appraisal, the entities are accredited, and the scope of their accredited work is designated by the conformity assessment body of a Federal Ministry.

EC agreements with third countries The Mutual Recognition Agreements on Conformity Assessment (MRAs) form the basis of the accreditation and designation of conformity assessment bodies. These agreements stipulate that the authority in the importing country recognizes the evaluation of devices or quality management systems conducted by a conformity assessment body located in the exporting country. This situation means that EU manufacturers can receive confirmation of compliance with third country regulations from EU conformity assessment bodies. The agreements imply the mutual acceptance of conformity assessment bodies and systems. They do not however imply mutual recognition (harmonization) of regulation. Thus, the regulations of the importing contract party apply.

MRA with the United States

The Agreement on Mutual Recognition with the United States of America was signed with the EU on May 18, 1998, and came into effect June 22, 1998. The texts of the agreement and further information can be found on the EU website, http://trade.ec.europa.eu/doclib/docs/2003/october/tradoc_11171 8.pdf. All conformity assessment bodies accredited are obliged to participate in the confidence- building exercises and in the national MRA information exchange. This information exchange of the notified bodies is in accordance with the Medical Devices Law (EK- Med). Recognized conformity assessment bodies

Product Certification

To sell products on the EU market of 27 Member States, as well as Norway, Liechtenstein and Iceland, U.S. exporters are required to apply CE marking whenever their product is covered by specific product legislation. CE marking product legislation offers manufacturers a number of choices and requires decisions to determine which safety/health concerns need to be addressed, which conformity assessment module is best suited to the manufacturing process, and whether or not to use EU-wide harmonized standards.

Organizations responsible for testing and certification are, for example, Underwriters Laboratories or the "Technischer Überwachungsverein e.V. - TÜV" (Technical Inspection Association). TÜVs are private companies set up by various German states to inspect and test products for compliance with German safety standards. Individual TÜVs have also been authorized by the German Government to test products for compliance with EU legislation and many have established representative offices in the United States. Within the DIN group, certification services are offered by: DIN CERTCO (product and services certification), and DQS (management systems). For the VDE (Association for Electrical, Electronic & Information Technologies) mark, which is applicable for electrical products only, companies can obtain information directly from the VDE (www.vde.com). The process for "VDE" certification is the same as that of the "GS" mark. Firms interested in certification should contact a U.S.-based test laboratory or a Conformity Assessment Body.

Self-Certification

For certain products, self-certification by manufacturers (through a Manufacturer's Declaration of Conformity) is sufficient.

Agreements on Certification

CB - IEC System for Conformity Testing to Standards for safety of electrical equipment.

CCA - CENELEC Certification Agreement.

CECC - CENELEC Electronic Components Committee - System for electronic components of assessed quality.

ENEC - ENEC Agreement.

HAR - CENELEC Agreement for the use of an agreed marking for cables and cords in combination with harmonized standards.

IECQ - IEC System for the quality assessment of electronic components and associated materials.

Accreditation

Independent certification bodies, known as notified bodies, have been officially accredited by competent authorities to test and certify to EU requirements. However, under U.S.-EU Mutual Recognition Agreements (MRAs), notified bodies based in the United States and referred to as conformity assessment bodies, are allowed to test in the United States to EU specifications, and vice versa. The costs are significantly lower which results in U.S. products becoming more competitive. At this time, the U.S.-EU MRAs cover the following sectors: Electromagnetic Compatibility (in force), Radio and telecommunications terminal equipment (in force), medical devices (in transition), pharmaceutical (on hold), recreational craft (in force) and marine equipment (in force).

The U.S. Department of Commerce, National Institute of Standards and Technology (NIST), has a link on its website to American and European Conformity Assessment bodies operating under a mutual recognition agreement. The German Accreditation Council (DAR) is a working group established in 1991 by ministries of the German Federal Government, ministries of the German federal states, and by representatives of the German industry. The DAR coordinates the activities in the field of accreditation and recognition of laboratories, certification, and inspection bodies as far as they are represented in the DAR; it represents German interests in national, European and international organizations dealing with general issues of accreditation and recognition, including voluntary and mandatory (KOGB) areas. The DAR itself does not carry out any accreditations or recognitions. All accreditation bodies represented in the DAR are operating on the basis of the EN 45000/EN ISO/IEC 17000 standard series and the DAR resolutions. With permission of the DAR, they may therefore use DAR certificates for accreditation.

Labeling and Marking

Manufacturers should be mindful that, in addition to the EU's mandatory and voluntary schemes, national voluntary labeling schemes might still apply. These schemes may be highly appreciated by consumers, and thus, become unavoidable for marketing purposes. Manufacturers are advised to take note that all labels require metric units although dual labeling is also acceptable. The use of language on labels has been the subject of a Commission Communication, which encourages multilingual information, while preserving the right of Member States to require the use of language of the country of consumption.

The EU Metric Directive (80/181/EEC), scheduled to go into effect January 1, 2010, has been modified to allow the continuation of both supplemental (U.S. customary, inch-pound) and metric units for consumer goods sold in the EU. The EU Eco-label EU legislation in 1992, revised in 2000, distinguishes environmentally friendly products and services through a voluntary labeling scheme called the Eco-label. Currently, the scheme applies to 7 product groups: cleaning products, appliances, paper products, clothing, lubricants, home and garden products and tourism services. The symbol, a green flower, is a voluntary mark.

The Eco-label is awarded to producers who can show that their product is less harmful to the environment than similar products. This "green label" also aims to encourage consumers to buy green products. However, the scheme does not establish ecological standards that all manufacturers are required to meet to place product on the market. Products without the EU Eco-label can still enter the EU as long as they meet the existing health, safety, and environmental standards and Regulations. The EU Eco-label is a costly scheme (up to EUR 1,300 for registration and up to EUR 25,000/year for the use of the label, with a reduction of 25% for SMEs) and has therefore not been widely used so far. However, the Eco-label can be a good marketing tool and, given the growing demand for green products in Europe, it is likely that the Eco-label will become more and more a reference for green consumers.

Agricultural Products

General Veterinary Requirements

In April 1997, the U.S. and the EU reached an equivalency agreement on an overall framework for recognizing each other's veterinary inspection systems. The veterinary equivalency agreement covers more than USD 1.5 billion in U.S. animal product exports to the EU and an equal value of EU exports to the United States. The agreement preserved most pre-existing trade in products, such as pet food, dairy, and egg products. All beef and pork exported to Germany for human consumption must come from slaughterhouses, cutting plants, and cold stores approved for export to the EU. Since 1989, the EU has prohibited imports of beef from cattle treated with growth hormones. Soon after this ban went into effect, an agreement was reached between the United States and the EU that allows

American producers of beef from animals not treated with hormones to export to the EU under certain conditions.

Beef

The EU beef market is largely insulated from the world market by high import duties. Import opportunities do exist, however, for selected products that are covered by fixed, relatively low tariffs or special quota. Most notably, the EU grants market access through a quota for annual imports of up to 11,500 MT of high-quality beef (HQB) from the United States and Canada. Beef entering the EU under the HBQ tariff-rate quota are subject to a 20 percent duty. In addition, starting in 2009, an autonomous tariff quota for high quality beef at zero percent duty was established for up to 20,000 MT per July/June marketing year.

Pork

Selected market opportunities exist for imports of pork. Market access within the EU has improved through the creation of a tariff-rate quota (TRQ) totaling 67,869 MT. The TRQ includes a 40,265 MT allocation for tenderloins, boneless loins and boneless hams. In addition, a 4,722 MT TRQ is reserved for boneless loins and boneless hams from the United States. Poultry: Unfortunately, U.S. and EU negotiators have not been able to reach agreement on a number of important points during the veterinary equivalency negotiations, particularly in the poultry sector. The most contentious issue is the use of pathogen reduction treatments in U.S. poultry processing. Most forms of anti-microbial treatments are prohibited in the EU. The EU's ban on anti-microbial treatments effectively blocks U.S. poultry exports to the EU, which were estimated at USD 50 million in 1996.

Dairy Products

The veterinary agreement allows for U.S. dairy products export to Germany and the EU from approved establishments under a fixed tariff.

Pet food

U.S. pet food exports to the EU must comply with EU regulation 1774/2002. This regulation, implemented in 2004, requires that animal by-products used in the production of feeds and pet food be derived from the carcasses of animals declared fit for human consumption following veterinary inspection. Provisions include a ban on intra-species recycling, fallen stock and restrictions on yellow grease. Certain categories of pet food have to be denatured with specified substances. Pet food plants have to be dedicated to the production of product fit for human consumption.

Plant Health

As part of the Single Market exercise, plant health regulations in the 27 European Union Member States have been harmonized. The regulations went into effect on June 1, 1993, for the 15 members then in the EU and in 2004 for the new accession countries. The EU has been successful in reducing the number of phytosanitary restrictions and new marketing opportunities have been created for U.S. horticultural exports. Phytosanitary certificates are required for many imported fresh products. With respect to the use of solid wooden packing materials (SWPM), it is important to note that the EU requires that all SWPM be either heat treated or fumigated beginning July 1, 2009. In addition to these treatment requirements, the material has to be free of bark. EU scientists fear that improperly treated SWPM is at risk for re-infestation. International plant protection standards as agreed upon by the United States do not require the absence of bark. Exporters should carefully follow the status of EU import requirements to avoid problems at the EU port of entry. Horticultural Products:

Germany is an important market for United States horticultural products. Principal products include almonds, walnuts, pistachios, prunes, raisins, citrus, and pears. Horticultural products entering Germany face a number of import restrictions. In addition to considerable tariffs that vary by product, imports of selected produce (tomatoes, cucumber, artichokes, zucchini squash, citrus, table grapes, apples, pears, apricots, cherries, peaches, nectarines and plums) are subject to an entry price system. Under such a system, imports that have a price at or above the respective entry price are assessed only the appropriate ad valorem duty. Imports, which have a price below, but within a certain range of the entry price, are assessed the ad valorem duty plus a specific duty that is the difference between the import price and the entry price. "Within a certain range" generally means within eight percent of the entry price. Imports having a price more than 8% below the entry price are assessed the ad valorem duty plus a very large specific duty (known as the tariff equivalent) which generally takes the cost of the product (import price plus duties) far above the entry price.

Organic Product

Until 2008 the German organic market had been growing at near double digital rates annually. In 2009, this growth leveled off as demand for organic products in conventional food stores decreased by several percentage points. Sales through specialized organic food stores are still increasing. The share of organic production in German agriculture is estimated to be about five percent. There are currently two regulations for organics in the EU, one for standards and one for imports. Implementation of the new import regulation framework for organic products started on January 1, 2009. Previously imported products had to be checked by the Member State for each individual product in an import authorization procedure. Under the new regulation, in countries such as the U.S. that are not on the equivalency list, products can be certified by control bodies. These control bodies must be directly approved for by the EU Commission. There is a transition period where it is still possible to import organic products through the old system. This possibility ends on January 1, 2013.

Consumer-Ready Product

Imports of consumer-ready food products into Germany face many market access restrictions and very strict food laws. In addition to bound import duties, the EU has established a complex system of border protection measures for food products. Depending on the world market situation for basic agricultural commodities, such as dairy products, sugar and cereals the EU mechanism of flexible tariffs may require variable import duties to protect European consumer-ready food products from imports made with lower-price inputs. Therefore, at many times processed products entering the EU are subject to additional import charges based on the percentage of sugar, milk fat, milk protein, and starch contained in the product. These additional import charges have made many imported processed food products non- competitive in the EU market.

Packaging Disposal

With the tremendous increase in waste and disposal problems, Germany has established legislation that contains certain rules for the disposal of packaging materials. In response to this legislation, a cooperative effort for the collection and recycling of packaging materials was initiated. The organization involved is called the "Duales System Deutschland" and it administers the use of the "Green Dot," a recycling symbol that is found on the packaging material of virtually all products sold in Germany.

While packaging materials for products sold in Germany are not legally required to carry the Green Dot, it is almost impossible to market a product in Germany without it. Typically, the importer pays a license fee to the user of the Green Dot, depending on the type and amount of packaging, and provides the exporter with the information necessary. In 2003, German retailers began requesting a deposit for disposable or "one-way" drink packages, i.e., soft drink or beer cans. Since the requested deposit is about three times as high as that requested for returnable beer bottles, it could disadvantage imported drinks. U.S. Agricultural Commodity Associations Active in Germany A number of U.S. agricultural commodity and other trade associations conduct market development programs in Germany. In some cases, these associations maintain field offices in Germany, while others may have a trade representative or public relations company representing their interests. Others may cover Germany from elsewhere in Europe or from offices in the United States. The USDA-operated Market Access Program (MAP) and Foreign Market Development program (FMD) provides a portion of the funding for the market development programs of these associations.

Chapter 5: Investment Climate

Openness to, and Restrictions upon, Foreign Investment The German government and industry actively encourage foreign investment in Germany, and German law provides foreign investors national treatment. Under German law, foreign-owned companies registered in the Federal Republic of Germany as a GmbH (limited liability company) or an AG (joint stock company) are treated no differently from German-owned companies.

Germany also treats foreigners equally in privatizations. There are no special nationality requirements on directors or shareholders, nor do investors need to register investment intent with any government entity except in the case of acquiring a significant stake in a firm in the defense or encryption industries. The investment-related problems foreign companies face are generally the same as for domestic firms, for example high marginal income tax rates and labor laws that impede hiring and dismissals. The German government has begun to address many of these problem areas through its reform programs. German courts have a good record in upholding the sanctity of contracts. The 1956 U.S.-FRG Treaty of Friendship, Commerce and Navigation affords U.S. investors national treatment and provides for the free movement of capital between the U.S. and Germany. Germany subscribes to the OECD Committee on Investment and Multinational Enterprises' (CIME) National Treatment Instrument and the OECD Code on Capital Movements and Invisible Transactions (CMIT).

While Germany's Foreign Economic Law contains a provision permitting restrictions on private direct investment flows in either direction for reasons of foreign policy, foreign exchange, or national security, no such restrictions have been imposed in practice. In such general cases, the federal government would first consult with the Bundesbank and the governments of the federal states. Specific legislation requiring government screening of foreign equity   acquisitions of 25% or more of German armaments companies took effect in July 2004.

Under the 2004 law, foreign entities that wish to purchase more than 25% equity in German manufacturers of armaments or cryptographic equipment are required to notify the Federal Economics and Technology Ministry, which then has one month in which to veto the sale. The transaction is regarded as approved if the Economics and Technology Ministry does not react in that time. The German government expanded the scope of the law in 2005 to include tank and tracked-vehicle engines.

A 2009 amendment to the Foreign Economic Law requires the German government to examine and potentially prohibit the acquisition of German companies of any size or sector by non-EU investors if they intend to buy more than 25% of the company's shares in cases where a threat to national security or public order is perceived. According to the American Chamber of Commerce in Germany, no foreign companies have complained so far about difficulties under the amendment. Germany ranks 15th in the Transparency International

Corruption Perception Index (CPI) that compares 178 countries worldwide (rank 1 being the country with least corruption).

Conversion and Transfer Policies

As a result of European Economic and Monetary Union (EMU), the Deutsche Mark (DM) was phased out on January 1, 2002, and replaced by the euro, which is a freely traded currency with no restrictions on transfer or conversion and which is the unit of currency in Germany and 16 other European countries. There is no difficulty in obtaining foreign exchange. There are also no restrictions on inflows and outflows of funds for remittances of profits or other purposes. Expropriation and Compensation German law provides that private property can be expropriated for public purposes only in a non-discriminatory manner and in accordance with established principles of constitutional and international law. There is due process and transparency of purpose, and investors and lenders to expropriated entities receive prompt, adequate and effective compensation.

Investment disputes concerning U.S. or other foreign investors and Germany are rare. Germany is a member of the International Center for the Settlement of Investment Disputes (ICSID), as well as a member of the 1958 New York Convention on the Recognition and Enforcement of Foreign Arbitral Awards. German courts are fully available for foreign investors in the event of investment disputes. The government does not interfere in the court system and accepts binding arbitration.

Performance Requirements and Incentives

European Union, federal and state authorities offer a broad range of incentive programs for investors in Germany. Cash Grants under the Joint Task for the Improvement of Regional Economic Structures, a program administered by the Ministry of Economics and Technology, is one available instrument for improving the infrastructure of regional economies and the economy as a whole – a primary objective of the German federal and state governments.

A comprehensive package of federal and state investment incentives, including cash, labor-related, and R&D incentives, interest-reduced loans, and public guarantees is available to domestic and foreign investors. In some cases, there may be performance requirements tied to the incentive, such as employment creation and maintaining a certain level of employment for a prescribed length of time. There are no requirements for local sourcing, export percentage, or local national ownership. Germany is in compliance with its WTO TRIMS obligations. The government has emphasized investment promotion in the states of the former East Germany and offers several programs only in these regions.

The major program is the Investment Allowance Act, which provides tax incentives for investments in the eastern states in the form of tax-free cash payments or tax credits. With the beginning of the current budgetary period of the EU, which started in January 2007 (and runs through 2013), Germany is to receive a total of EUR 26.3 billion. The German states located in the former East Germany received the majority of the EU subsidies allocated to Germany, EUR 15.1 billion, for the budget period of 2007-2013. Foreign investors are generally subject to the same eligibility conditions as German investors for incentive programs.

Programs in Germany

Investment grants: Cash incentives in the form of non-repayable grants usually based on investment costs or assumed wage costs. Incentives vary according to the economic development level of the region, with up to 30 percent of eligible expenditures channeled to large enterprises, 40 percent to medium-sized enterprises and 50 percent to small enterprises.

Credit Programs

Loans at below-market interest rates from the KfW banking group and state development banks, partially targeting small and medium sized enterprises (SMEs). Public guarantees: Public guarantees for companies which do not have the collateral that private-sector banks ordinarily require. Labor-related incentives: Support from 800 local job centers, programs focus on recruitment support, pre-hiring training, wage subsidies, and on-the-job training. R&D Incentives: R&D grants, reduced-interest loans, and special partnership programs provided by the EU, the German government and German state governments.

Foreign investors can obtain more information on investment conditions and incentives from: Germany Trade and Invest is the foreign trade and investment agency of the Federal Republic of Germany, formed by the merger of Invest in Germany with the German Office for Foreign Trade in January 2009. American companies can, with effort, generally obtain the resident visas and spouse work permits they require to do business in Germany, but the relevant laws are quite broad and considerable administrative discretion is exercised in their application. A number of U.S. states have not yet concluded reciprocal agreements with the German government to recognize one another's driver's licenses. As a result, licenses from those states are not usable in Germany for longer than six months, whereas licenses from states that have signed agreements can be converted to German licenses after six months.

Right to Private Ownership and Establishment

Foreign and domestic entities have the right to establish and own business enterprises, engage in all forms of remunerative activity, and acquire and dispose of interests in business enterprises.

Protection of Property Rights

The German Government adheres to a policy of national treatment, which considers property owned by foreigners as fully protected under German law. There is almost no discrimination against foreign investment and foreign acquisition, ownership, control or disposal of property or equity interests, with airline ownership being an exception based on EU regulations, which require an EU majority ownership of shares to obtain an operating permit as an EU airline. In Germany, the concept of mortgages is subject to a recognized and reliable security. Secured interests in property, both chattel and real, are recognized and enforced. Intellectual property is well protected by German laws.

Germany is a member of the World Intellectual Property Organization (WIPO). Germany is also a party to the major international intellectual property protection agreements: the Bern Convention for the Protection of Literary and Artistic Works, the Paris Convention for the Protection of Industrial Property, the Universal Copyright Convention, the Geneva Phonograms Convention, the Patent Cooperation Treaty, the Brussels Satellite Convention, and the Treaty of Rome on Neighboring Rights. National treatment is also granted foreign copyright holders, including remuneration for private recordings. Under the TRIPS agreement, the federal government also grants legal protection for practicing U.S. artists against the commercial distribution of unauthorized live recordings in Germany.

Germany has signed the WIPO Internet treaties and ratified them in 2003. Foreign and German rights holders, however, remain critical of provisions in the German Copyright Act that allow exceptions for private copies of copyrighted works. Most rights holder organizations regard German authorities' enforcement of intellectual property protections as sufficient, although problems persist due to lenient court rulings in some cases and the difficulty of combating piracy of copyrighted works on the Internet. In 2008, Germany implemented the EU enforcement directive with a national bill, thereby strengthening the privileges of rights holders and allowing for improved enforcement action.

Transparency of the Regulatory System
Germany has transparent and effective laws and policies to promote competition, including anti-trust laws. In recent years,

German authorities lifted many restrictions on store business hours, which had formerly restrained competition and business opportunities. There are concerns in Germany and abroad about the level of regulation prevailing with regulatory authority dispersed over the federal, state, and local levels. Many investors consider Germany's bureaucracy excessive, which has prompted most state governments to establish investment promotion offices and investment banks to expedite the process. New rules have simplified bureaucratic requirements, but industry must sometimes contend with officials' relative inexperience with deregulation and lingering pro-regulation attitudes.

In response to the problem, the federal government continues to reduce bureaucracy. In 2006, the National Regulatory Control Council was established, tasked with assessing the impact of regulatory law and encouraging the federal government to cut red tape. The council reports annually and recommends further measures. The federal government also set the target of reducing the costs of law-induced bureaucracy by 25 percent by 2011. Economics Minister Rainer Brüderle (pro-market FDP) seems to be very interested in reducing the bureaucratic burden and has moved the section within the Economics Ministry dealing with bureaucracy reform closer to his own office.

Germany now uses the Standard Cost Model to quantify and identify bureaucratic costs in every new legislative proposal. This provides increased transparency about the   amount of time and cost that companies and citizens have to spend because of bureaucratic requirements. The German National Regulatory Control Council estimates that applying the Standard Cost Model has reduced bureaucratic costs for companies by 3.5 billion euro in the past four years, measured against the bureaucratic burden that was in effect before the new, improved legislation. Laws and regulations in Germany are routinely published in draft, and public comments are solicited. The legal, regulatory and accounting systems can be complex but are transparent and consistent with international norms.

Efficient Capital Markets and Portfolio Investment

Germany has a modern financial sector but is often considered "over-banked," as evidenced by on-going consolidation and low profit margins. The country's so-called "three-pillar" banking system, made up of private commercial banks, state-owned and cooperative banks, and savings banks, survived the global financial crisis, but pressures to consolidate are increasing. To improve their international competitiveness, the larger, privately-owned banks in particular have launched massive cost-cutting programs. Germany's eight regional state-owned banks ("Landesbanken") were among the hardest hit by the crisis. Passing grades on stress tests in summer 2010 have erased few doubts about the need for an overhaul of the sector. Chinese investors are negotiating partial stakes in several state-owned banks.

The EU Competition Commissioner attached tough downsizing conditions in exchange for approving federal and state government bailout packages. The financial crisis also triggered the take-over of Dresdner Bank by Commerzbank and that of Postbank by Deutsche Bank. This has effectively reduced the number of top German privately owned banks to just two. In the midst of the financial crisis, the German government created a Financial Market Stabilization Fund ("SoFFin") which had the ability to offer guarantees up to 400 billion euros and purchase assets for an additional 80 billion euros. The two most prominent recipients of rescue funds were Commerzbank (its take-over of Dresdner Bank brought it to the brink of bankruptcy) and Hypo Real Estate (HRE). In the case of HRE, the government departed from long-standing tradition and nationalized the bank in order to prevent a breakdown of the German (and European) covered-bond market – a backbone of German real estate financing. The law permitting the expropriation of HRE was designed for that institution only and expired in June 2009. There are several court cases pending in which the government's action of "squeezing out" HRE's previous owners is being challenged.

One such high-profile case is that of U.S. private equity firm, J. C. Flowers, which led a consortium of investors that owned nearly 25 percent of the troubled bank prior to nationalization. The government argued that without its actions, HRE would have become insolvent, and owners would have lost their assets anyway. At 1.30 euros per share, the German Government paid an estimated 10 cents more than the market value of HRE stock, though JC Flowers believes this was too little. SoFFin also created two "bad banks" with toxic assets from West LB and HRE, respectively. Credit is available at market-determined rates to both domestic and foreign investors, and a variety of credit instruments are available.

Legal, regulatory and accounting systems are generally transparent and consistent with international banking norms, but in light of global financial turmoil, Germany is pushing for even more transparency in international financial markets. Germany has a universal banking system regulated by federal authorities. The German Bundesbank and the government have rebutted concerns that the economic crisis, in connection with tougher capital requirements for banks mandated in the G-20, could lead to a shortage of credit in the German economy. The government has taken action to further mitigate the situation by offering additional state financing options through its state lender KfW. Given the prevailing overall economic conditions, mergers and acquisitions (M&A) have decreased in recent years in line with global trends.

Prior to the global financial crisis, Germany had seen an upswing in M&A transactions due to improved economic conditions, the increased financial assets of the top 30 companies listed in the German stock exchange (DAX), and the high value of the euro. "Cross shareholding" exists among some large German companies, in particular among banks that hold shares in large industrial customers. However, Germany's major banks have been reducing their cross-shareholdings in recent years.

In response to a 2004 EU directive, the government has implemented legislation establishing new rules to ensure greater transparency in takeovers. The new law went into effect in 2006. In recent years, Germany has implemented a series of laws to improve its securities trading system, including laws against insider trading and the Fourth Financial Market Promotion Law in 2003. In 2002, a corporate governance code was adopted which, while voluntary, requires listed companies to "comply or explain" why the code or parts thereof have not been followed. The code is intended to increase transparency and improve management response to shareholder concerns. The Finance and Justice Ministries drew up a ten-point plan in 2003 to improve investor protection. As a part of that plan, the government tabled a bill in November 2004 that would (a) increase the liability of boards of directors for false or misleading statements; and (b) improve oversight of auditing operations.

The EU's Financial Services Action Plan – an effort intended to create a more integrated European financial market by 2005 – has helped stimulate changes in the German regulatory framework, including adoption of International Accounting Standards for listed firms and use of company investment prospects on an EU-wide basis. In 2008, Germany passed legislation that makes private equity firms subject to greater transparency rules, including the publication of a business plan for the acquired company.

Competition from State-Owned Enterprises
State-owned or partially state-owned enterprises still exist in several sectors, most importantly in railroads, postal services, telecommunications and the banking sector. Privatization of state-owned utilities has promoted competition and led to falling prices in some sectors. Following the deregulation of the telecommunications sector in 1998, scores of foreign and domestic companies invested vast sums in that sector. In the fixed-line telecommunications market, Deutsche Telekom (DT) competitors currently account for an overall market share of more than 21 percent, while in the broadband market,

competitors providing DSL-broadband constitute around 41 percent. In June 2004, a new telecommunications law to implement EU directives entered into force. The law mandates less regulation in some areas while giving the regulator new powers to   address abuse of market dominance and ensure competitors' access to services.

A second amendment to the telecommunications law became effective in early 2007. Aimed at strengthening consumer rights, it also includes a controversial component entitling Deutsche Telekom to a regulatory holiday in return for a sizeable investment in a VDSL network, providing the investment creates a "new market." However, in 2009 the European Court of Justice ruled that the regulatory holiday granted to DT infringes on European law. The German government never applied the regulatory holiday and announced that it plans to abolish the provision with the upcoming reform of the telecommunications law, which will implement the December 2009 EU telecoms package.

The German government continues to hold a 32% share in DT, although it has expressed its intention to sell these shares "eventually." The government partially privatized Deutsche Post (DP) in November 2000 and has stated its intentions eventually to divest its remaining shares. It currently holds a 30.5% share in DP. After successive rounds of liberalization, DP's monopoly on standard letter mail delivery expired on December 31, 2007, even though DP has remained the dominant player in that market. Two significant barriers to entry adversely affecting competition have recently been dismantled. 1) In January 2010, the German

Federal Administrative Court ruled that the minimum wage in the postal sector, imposed by the government in 2007, is no longer valid; competitors commended the decision, as they regarded the minimum wage as favoring Deutsche Post. 2) Value-added Tax (VAT) exemption (of 19%), which DP received for offering universal service, was abolished by the German government in early 2010, following a verdict by the European Court of Justice. Since July 2010, prices for DP business and bulk mail include VAT. VAT exemption now only applies for services used by individual consumers, such as over-the-counter parcels. Competitors are also entitled to VAT exemption if they offer universal service. Germany's Cartel Office and Germany's other regulatory agencies seek to address problems and settle complaints brought forward by foreign market entrants and bidders.

However, as noted above, German law and court decisions have limited these agencies' jurisdiction in some areas. The planned sale to private investors of just under 25% of the 100% government-owned railway Deutsche Bahn (DB) did not take place and is unlikely to take place in the foreseeable future. A series of data privacy scandals forced the DB CEO to resign in 2009, when DB also started to have serious safety problems with high-speed, freight and Berlin light rail rolling stock, primarily due to lack of maintenance. DB was accused of attempting to cut costs to improve its attractiveness for privatization, at the expense of safety and reliability.

These accusations and the financial crisis led the government to halt privatization efforts in early 2010. In 2010/11 the second consecutive severe winter again caused chaos in the Berlin light rail passenger system as well as service restrictions and delays to the regional and long-haul services. Technical problems, poor rolling stock and infrastructure maintenance remain concerns. In January 2011 the new DB CEO stated that it will take four to five years and heavy investment to return the German domestic rail service to reliability.

Three different types of banks exist in Germany: privately-owned banks, state-owned banks (Landesbanken) and cooperative banks. The Landesbanken used to have advantages over privately-owned banks in obtaining credit. Under the pressure of Germany's privately-owned banks, the EU forced an end to these advantages in 2005. This means that the Landesbanken can no longer raise money cheaply with AAA ratings   based on a government guarantee. At the moment, foreign banks need not fear unfair competition from state-owned or cooperative banks. The greater part of the German energy sector is in private hands.

Analysts say the government initially supported Germany's oligopolistic energy providers' opposition to the 1998 EU Liberalization Directive and the 2000 EU Gas Market Liberalization Directive. The electricity market nevertheless slowly opened to competition. The gas sector proved more resistant but is now opening. After EU pressure, the Federal Network Agency (BNA) started regulating power transmission prices and grid access in 2006 and pipeline access and transport prices in the gas sector in 2007. Rising prices and growing earnings in the energy sector have caused consumer anger and have increased political pressure on the industry to rein in prices and improve market transparency. The government has strengthened the operative rights of the Cartel Office in the energy sector and introduced legislation to enhance entry to the market. BNA continues to reduce administrative hurdles in the gas sector. After years of competitive stagnation, some new foreign competitors have entered the power market and have begun to move into the gas market.

Corporate Social Responsibility (CSR)

The Federal Ministry of Labor and Social Affairs is the leading ministry for CSR within the German government. In early October 2010, at the suggestion of the Ministry of Labor and Social Affairs, the Federal Cabinet approved an Action Plan for CSR aimed at anchoring CSR more firmly in enterprises and public bodies, winning over even more small and medium-sized enterprises (SMEs) for CSR and increasing the visibility and credibility of CSR. The Action Plan is based on recommendations of the National CSR Forum, which consists of 44 experts from business, unions, non-governmental organizations and academia. The forum has advised the Labor Ministry since early 2009 on the development of a National CSR Strategy. On the business side, the American Chamber of Commerce in Germany (AmCham Germany) is active in upholding the standards of social responsibility within the realm of their members' corporate business. AmCham Germany issues regular publications on companies' CSR approaches. Its committee on corporate social responsibility serves as a platform to exchange best practices, identify trends and discuss regulatory initiatives.

Political Violence

Political acts of violence against either foreign or domestic business enterprises are extremely rare. Isolated cases of violence directed at certain minorities and asylum seekers have not affected U.S. investments or investors.

Corruption

Among industrialized countries, Germany ranks in the middle, according to Transparency International's corruption indices. The construction and health sectors and public contracting, in conjunction with undue political party influence and party donations, represent areas of continued concern. Nevertheless, U.S. firms have not identified corruption as an impediment to investment. The German government has sought to reduce domestic and foreign corruption. Strict anti-corruption laws apply to domestic economic activity, and the laws are enforced. Germany ratified the 1998 OECD Anti-Bribery Convention in February 1999, thereby criminalizing bribery of foreign public officials by German citizens and firms. The necessary tax reform legislation ending the tax write-off for bribes in Germany and abroad became law in March 1999.

Anti-Corruption

Convention but has not yet ratified it. The country participates in the relevant EU anti- corruption measures. Germany has increased penalties for bribery of German officials, for corrupt practices between companies, and for price-fixing by companies competing for public contracts. It has also strengthened anti-corruption provisions on support extended by the official export credit agency and has tightened the rules for public tenders. Most state governments and local authorities have contact points for whistle- blowing and provisions for rotating personnel in areas prone to corruption.

However, not all state governments have prosecutors specialized in corruption. Government officials are forbidden from accepting gifts linked to their jobs. Transparency Deutschland, the German Chapter of Transparency International, considers its main goals in Germany to be a national corruption register and speedy ratification of the UN Anti-Corruption Convention, placing bribery of parliamentarians on the same level as bribery of public officials. Draft legislation to create a national corruption register failed to win the approval of the federal states in 2005, but some individual states maintain their own registers. Federal freedom of information legislation entered into force in January 2006, but many regard the government's handling as restrictive. Several states have their own freedom of information laws.

The German government has successfully prosecuted hundreds of domestic corruption cases over the years. Few charges were filed for bribery of foreign government officials in the first years after the OECD Anti-Bribery Convention came into force in 1999. However, the U.S. Securities and Exchange Commission (SEC) investigations into Siemens and Daimler and the heavy fines imposed on the two companies focused public attention on foreign bribery from 2007 onwards. The issue is likely to remain in the headlines – German court proceedings against the first former Siemens Board members are due to start soon, and the SEC is reportedly also investigating former Siemens managers.

In 2009 German prosecutors initiated seven new cases, while 20 were resolved.

Bilateral Investment Agreements

Germany has investment treaties in force with 131 countries and territories. Of these, eight are with "predecessor" states (including Czechoslovakia, the Soviet Union, and Yugoslavia) and are indicated with asterisks.

Treaties are in force with the following states and territories: Afghanistan; Albania; Algeria; Angola; Antigua and Barbuda; Argentina; Armenia; Azerbaijan; Bahrain; Bangladesh; Barbados; Belarus; Benin; Bolivia; Bosnia and Herzegovina; Botswana; Burkina Faso; Brunei; Bulgaria; Burundi; Cambodia; Cameroon; Cape Verde; Central African Republic; Chad; Chile; China (People's Republic); Congo (Republic); Congo (Democratic Republic); Costa Rica; Croatia; Cuba; Czechoslovakia**; Czech Republic*; Dominica; Ecuador; Egypt; El Salvador; Estonia; Ethiopia; Gabon; Georgia; Ghana; Greece; Guatemala; Guinea; Guyana; Haiti; Honduras; Hong Kong; Hungary; India; Indonesia; Iran; Ivory Coast; Jamaica; Jordan; Kazakhstan; Kenya; Republic of Korea; Kuwait; Kyrgyzstan*; Laos; Latvia; Lebanon; Lesotho; Liberia; Libya; Lithuania; Macedonia; Madagascar; Malaysia; Mali; Malta; Mauritania; Mauritius; Mexico; Moldova*; Mongolia; Morocco; Mozambique; Namibia; Nepal; Nicaragua; Niger; Nigeria; Oman; Pakistan; Panama; Papua New Guinea; Paraguay; Peru; Philippines; Poland; Portugal; Qatar; Romania; Russia*; Rwanda; Saudi Arabia; Senegal; Sierra Leone; Singapore; Slovak Republic*; Slovenia; Somalia; South Africa; Soviet Union**; Sri Lanka; St. Lucia; St.

Vincent and the Grenadines; Serbia; Sudan; Swaziland; Syria; Tajikistan*; Tanzania; Thailand; Togo; Trinidad & Tobago; Tunisia; Turkey; Turkmenistan; Uganda; Ukraine; United Arab Emirates; Uruguay; Uzbekistan; Venezuela; Vietnam; Yemen; Yugoslavia**; Zambia; and Zimbabwe.

(Note: * denotes treaty in force with predecessor state; ** denotes continued application of treaties with former entities, which has not been taken into account in regard to the total number of treaties.)

Taxation of U.S. firms within Germany is governed by the "Convention for the Avoidance of Double Taxation with Respect to Taxes on Income." It has been in effect since 1989 (and, since January 1, 1991, for the area that comprised the former German Democratic Republic). With respect to income taxes, both countries agree to grant credit for their respective federal income taxes on taxes paid on profits by enterprises located in each other's territory.

The German system is more complex, but there are more similarities than differences between the German and U.S. business tax systems. The U.S. and Germany ratified the Protocol of June 1, 2006, amending their 1989 income tax treaty and protocol. The new protocol updates the existing treaty and includes several   changes, including a zero-rate provision for subsidiary-parent dividends, a more restrictive limitation-on-benefits provision, and a mandatory binding arbitration provision.

OPIC and Other Investment Insurance Programs

OPIC programs were available for the new states of eastern Germany following reunification for several years during the early 1990s but were suspended following progress in the economic and political transition.

Labor

The German labor force is generally highly skilled, well educated, disciplined, and very productive. The complex set of reforms of labor and social welfare institutions implemented under the former SPD/Green government contributed to overcoming structural weaknesses of the German welfare state and created an institutional structure more conducive to strong employment growth and lower unemployment. Additional reforms under Chancellor Merkel and a series of changes in collective bargaining in recent years have strengthened the forces driving economic growth. On the negative side, the very sacrifices that have made German products more competitive and helped the country outpace many of its European partners – strict wage controls, a retirement age rising to 67 from 65, lower welfare payments and eased hiring and firing – have resulted in a growing low-wage sector, declining domestic consumption and a deep feeling of insecurity.

In 2010, the German economy rebounded strongly. Despite suffering an economic contraction of 4.7% in 2009 – during which time unemployment doubled in the United States to 10.1% and approached 20% in Spain and Greece – Germany saw its unemployment rate fall to 7.4%, its lowest level in 17 years. While long-term unemployment remains high, it has started to decline, and the outlook for 2011 is even more promising. The eight leading economic think tanks now predict a 3.5% increase in GDP for 2010 and an estimated 2.5% for 2011. They also project wages to increase by 2.8% in 2011 and unemployment to drop below the politically sensitive three-million mark during the next 12 months.

As a result the jobless rate is expected to fall from 7.4% this year to an estimated 6.9% in 2011. Among the reasons behind the surprising resiliency of the labor market – in addition to the widespread use of government-funded short-time work programs and company working-time accounts – is the fact that many companies entered the recession with a capital cushion and deliberately decided to keep highly skilled labor in hopes of riding out the crisis. In addition, parts of the services sector (e.g., health and welfare, education and training) were not adversely affected by the recession and are continuing to create jobs. In July 2010, the Institute of Economic and Social Research presented its interim report on Germany's 2010 round of collective bargaining, which was strongly affected by the economic crisis. The study evaluated collective bargaining agreements concluded in the first half of 2010, which affect about 37% of all employees covered by collective bargaining. The average annual increase in wages and salaries was around 1.7% in 2010, well below the average of 2.6% in 2009.

There is still a considerable gap in earnings between men and women in Germany. Collective agreements concluded in the first half of 2010 did not include provisions to tackle wage discrimination and promote equal opportunity. Since the late 1990s, Germany's system of wage determination through multi-company, industry-wide contracts has become considerably more decentralized. Although sector- wide labor agreements can set wages and working conditions at high levels in some industries, company-level agreements frequently deviate from them. Many industry-wide contracts have been revised in recent years, not only to include highly flexible working time arrangements but also to introduce escape clauses for ailing companies, and to lower entrance pay scales and performance-based annual bonuses.

Moreover, the coverage of collective agreements has been declining. Multi-company, industry-wide contracts cover about 43.4% of all firms; 5.3% are covered by a company-level agreement; and 51.3% are not covered at all. Coverage in the eastern states is even lower than in the west: Collective bargaining agreements covered approximately 65 percent of the labor force in the western part of the country and approximately 51 percent in the East. Germany does not have a statutory minimum wage. However, binding minimum wages have been established in 16 sectors so far (e.g., construction, electrical trades, painting, mail, or waste management) covering an estimated two million workers.

In August 2010, new national minimum wages for caregivers came into force affecting about two-thirds of a total of 810,000 caregivers in Germany. The regulation will apply to all employees, regardless of the country of origin of their employer. In general, the current German government remains opposed to the introduction of a national legal minimum wage. However, since Germany has to open up its labor market to all European

Union nationals in May 2011, Labor Minister von der Leyen is calling for a minimum wage for temporary jobs in Germany to prevent eastern European workers in particular from undercutting salaries in certain service sectors. Germany's education system for skilled labor, combining on-the-job and in-school training for apprentices, produces many of the skills emplo

yers need. There are rigidities in the training system, however, such as restrictions on night work for apprentices, to which some employers object. Another criticism is that the system is inflexible with regard to occupational categories and training standards. Labor unions complain that employers do not establish enough training slots and do not hire enough of the trainees after their training is completed. While regulatory obstacles to workers' mobility are expected to decrease by May 2011, the alarming demographic trend in Germany has already led to serious labor shortages in many high-skilled fields, above all engineering, technical professions and manufacturing trades.

In addition, lathe operators, specialized metal workers, social workers, nurses and nursing home workers are in short supply. While trade union membership has continued to decline, there has been a notable slowdown in this development in recent years. About 21% of the workforce is organized into unions. The overwhelming majority are in eight unions largely grouped by industry or service sector. These unions are affiliates of the German Trade Union Federation (DGB). Several smaller unions exist outside the DGB, principally for white-collar professions. Since peaking at more than 13 million members shortly after

German re-unification, total DGB union membership has steadily declined to 6.3 million at the end of 2009. Unions' right to strike and employers' right to lock out are protected in the German constitution. Court rulings over the years, however, have limited management recourse to lockouts.

At the company level, works councils represent the interests of workers vis-à-vis their employers. A works council may be elected in all private companies employing at least five people. The rights of the works council include the right to be informed, to be consulted, and to participate in company decisions. Works councils often help labor and management to settle problems before they become disputes and disrupt work. "Codetermination" laws give the workforce in medium-sized or large companies (stock corporations, limited liability companies, partnerships limited by shares, co-operatives, and mutual insurance companies) significant voting representation on the firms' supervisory boards. This codetermination in the supervisory board extends to all company activities.

Foreign-Trade Zones / Free Trade Zones

There are five free trade zones in Germany established and operated under EU law: Bremerhaven, Cuxhaven, Deggendorf, Duisburg and Hamburg. These duty-free zones within the ports also permit value-added processing and manufacturing for EU-external markets, albeit with certain requirements. All of them are open to both domestic and foreign entities. In recent years falling tariffs and the progressive enlargement of the EU have gradually eroded much of the utility and attractiveness of duty-free zones. Kiel and Emden lost free trade zone status in 2010.

Chapter 6: Trade, Financing, and Travel

The majority of import transactions by German customers, especially those involving large German distributors, take place under seller-buyer terms, such as the common 30/60/90-day accounts, or payment against documents. The most popular payment mechanism by which German importers remit payment to their U.S. suppliers is the electronic funds transfer (EFT, equivalent to SWIFT or wire transfers), the fastest and cheapest way to transfer funds. Current technology makes online transfers reasonably secure and transparent.

The letter of credit is still used in some industry sectors but now covers a fraction of total imports, largely due to its cost and time requirements as well as the ease in obtaining credit ratings in Germany, which increases transparency and transactional safety. L/C's for payments under USD 5,000 are almost unknown in Germany. U.S. exporters may also encounter Bills of Exchange (Wechsel), usually payable within two or three months, but this antiquated payment mechanism is also passing from the scene.

Cash-in- advance is also rare in German import payment, although Germany's economic doldrums have recently led to an increase of financially strapped firms on whom such terms are imposed. Both private and public credit insurance are available in Germany. Euler Hermes, Coface and Atradius are among the private providers (which also offer ranking and scoring services); and the main public insurer is the Staatliche Kreditversicherung (Hermes-Buergschaften), which is administered by Euler

Hermes and is used to cover German exports to countries with high political and country risk. United States exporters tend to purchase credit insurance to a much lesser extent than European exporters due to the relatively greater recourse to factoring in the United States.

Overall, German firms continue to enjoy a relatively good reputation for their payment practices and management of credit. Critical industries for U.S. exporters are construction, furniture, paper and publishing. Default risk is somewhat higher for firms in unevenly performing eastern Germany. The U.S. Commercial Service Germany offers the International Company Profile as a tool to help evaluate the creditworthiness of potential customers or partners and recommends that U.S. exporters consider normal, prudent credit practices in Germany in all transactions.

The Export-Import Bank of the United States (Ex-Im Bank) is the official export credit agency of the United States. The Ex-Im Bank's mission is to assist in financing exports of U.S. goods and services to international markets. The Ex-Im Bank enables U.S. companies -- large and small -- to turn export opportunities into real sales that help to maintain and create U.S. jobs and contribute to a stronger national economy. The Ex-Im Bank does not compete with private-sector lenders but provides export-financing products that fill gaps in trade financing. The bank assumes credit and country risks that the private sector is unable or unwilling to accept and helps to level the playing field for U.S. firms by matching the financing that other governments provide to their exporters. The Ex-Im Bank provides working capital guarantees (pre-export financing); export credit insurance; and loan guarantees and direct loans (buyer financing). Primarily focusing on developing markets worldwide, Ex-Im Bank has recently supported U.S firms supplying one of the world's largest solar energy facilities, located in Bavaria.

The Banking System

Germany has a non-discriminatory, well developed financial services infrastructure. Germany's universal banking system allows the country's more than 39,000 bank offices not only to take deposits and make loans to customers but also to trade in securities. The traditional German system of cross-shareholding among banks and industry, as well as a high rate of bank borrowing relative to equity financing, allowed German banks to exert substantial influence on industry in the past. Private banks control roughly 30% of the market, while publicly owned savings banks partially linked to state and local governments account for 50% of banking transactions, and cooperative banks make up the balance. All three types of banks offer a full range of services to their customers. A state-owned bank, KfW, provides special credit services, including the financing of homeowner mortgages, guarantees to small and medium-sized businesses, financing for projects in disadvantaged regions in Germany and export financing for projects in developing countries. Regional state-owned banks ("Landesbanken") were among the hardest hit by the economic crisis and their future is uncertain.

The financial crisis also triggered a major consolidation of the German banking sector with Commerzbank buying up Dresdner Bank, Deutsche Bank taking over Postbank and UniCredit Bank buying up Hypovereinsbank. Virtually all major U.S. banks are represented in the German market, principally but not exclusively in the city of Frankfurt am Main, Germany's main financial center. Citibank, however, sold its retail banking business to Credit Mutuel of France in 2008. A large number of German banks, including some of the partially state-owned regional banks, similarly maintain subsidiaries, branches and/or representative offices in the United States. Practices regarding finance, availability of capital and schedules of payment are comparable to those that prevail in the United States. There are no restrictions or barriers on the movement of capital, foreign exchange earnings or dividends.

Project Financing

Germany possesses the financial framework and institutions to support the development of large infrastructure projects. However, the volume of project finance operations has been relatively modest in Germany in comparison to other EU countries, particularly the U.K. and France. Although the rising indebtedness of the German federal government and local authorities would seem to favor this type of financing, difficult economic conditions have also limited anticipated rates of return for potential project finance developers.

Other inhibiting factors are Germany's complex juridical and federal frameworks, which make project-financed works harder to structure than in other countries. One area that has attracted project finance, including that involving a few U.S. developers and investors, is alternative energy production. Clean and renewable energy projects generally have gained prominence in

Germany through the country's commitment to meeting sharply reduced CO_2 emission targets. The principal German institutions active in facilitating project finance deals are the state- owned KfW Bank Group (Kreditanstalt fuer Wiederaufbau), which plays a major role in virtually all industries, commercial banks such as the Commerzbank, and several of the publicly-owned savings banks controlled by state and local governments (Landesbanken) located in northern Germany. The KfW Group includes KfW IPEX-Bank, which supports a consortia with German members to design and finance infrastructure projects in Germany and overseas. Another group member, KfW Development Bank (Foerderbank), helps municipalities to finance infrastructure.

Business Customs

Never underestimate the importance of punctuality in German business culture. Arriving even five to ten minutes after the appointed time is perceived as late; a fifteen minute variance would be considered a very serious faux pas and could mean a shaky start to any potential business relations. Be prepared to make an appointment for most things. The preferred times for business appointments are between 10:00 a.m. and 1:00 p.m. or between 3:00 p.m. and 5:00 p.m. Avoid scheduling appointments on Friday afternoons, as some offices close by 2:00 p.m. or 3:00 p.m. on Fridays. Giving compliments is not part of German business protocol and can often cause embarrassment and awkwardness. Germans traditionally use: "Wie geht es Ihnen?" ["How are you?"] as a literal question that expects a literal answer, in contrast to the common English usage of "How's it going?" to simply meaning "Hi". It may, therefore, be considered strange or superficial to ask the question and keep on moving without waiting for an answer.

Travel

A passport is required. A visa is not required for tourist/business stays up to 90 days within the Schengen Group of countries, which includes Germany

Travel by plane, train or car meets international standards, but prices exceed U.S. averages. The number of in-country flights has been picking up and the train stations that dot the country provide sufficient access to nearly all cities. Nevertheless, cars are the most popular means of transport and Germany's famous highway system is extensive. Geographic distances are relatively short, when compared to the United States, but as Germany is much more densely populated than its European neighbors, it may take a little longer to travel the same distance in Germany than it may take in France or Scandinavia. Language German. In larger towns, many people can communicate in English.

When bringing professional equipment, such as electronic goods, cameras, and musical instruments, into Germany, it is strongly recommended that you first contact the consulate or embassy in your area for customs information. You might also want to consider purchasing an ATA Carnet. The ATA Carnet, which allows for the temporary, duty-free entry of goods into over 50 countries, is issued by the United States Council for International Business by appointment of the U.S. Voltage in Germany is 230. Electronic equipment from the U.S. will require an adaptor.

Health

Good medical care is widely available. Doctors and hospitals may expect immediate payment in cash for health services from tourists and persons with no permanent address in Germany. Most doctors, hospitals and pharmacies do not accept credit cards. Medical Insurance: The Department of State strongly urges Americans to consult with their medical insurance company prior to traveling abroad to confirm whether their policy applies overseas and if it will cover emergency expenses, such as a medical evacuation. U.S. medical insurance plans seldom cover health costs incurred outside the United States unless supplemental coverage is purchased.

Chapter 7: Contacts

Federal Ministry of Economics and Technology

Bundesministerium fuer Wirtschaft & Technologie

www.bmwi.de

Germany Trade and Invest

www.gtai.com

Federal Ministry of Finance

Bundesministerium der Finanzen

www.bundesfinanzministerium.de

Country Trade Associations/Chambers of Commerce

Bundesverband der Deutschen Industrie e.V. (BDI)

(Federation of German Industries)

www.bdi-online.de

Deutscher Industrie und Handelskammertag (DIHK)

(Federation of German Chambers of Industry and Commerce)

www.dihk.de

Bundesverband Grosshandel, Aussenhandel, Dienstleistungen
e.V.

(Federation of German Wholesale, Foreign Trade and Services)

www.bga.de

Zentralverband Elektrotechnik- und Eletronikindustrie e.V.

(ZVEI)

(German Electrical and Electronic Manufacturers Association)

www.zvei.de

Verband Deutscher Maschinen- und Anlagenbau e.V. (VDMA)

(German Association of Machinery and Plant Manufacturers)

www.vdma.org

Centralvereinigung Deutscher Wirtschaftsverbaende fuer

Handelsvermittlung und

Vertrieb (CDH)

(National Association of German Commercial Agencies and

Distributors)

www.cdh.de

Country Commercial Banks:

There are numerous domestic and foreign banks represented in

Germany; among the largest German institutions are:

Deutsche Bank AG

Commerzbank AG

www.deutsche-bank.de

www.commerzbank.com

Bayerische Hypo- und Vereinsbank AG

www.hypovereinsbank.de

Deutsche Postbank AG www.postbank.de

E. U.S. Embassy Trade Personnel

United States Embassy, Berlin www.usembassy.de

Commercial Service http://export.gov/germany/contact/berlin/

U.S. Consulates

Dusseldorf http://duesseldorf.usconsulate.gov

Commercial Service

http://export.gov/germany/Contact/Dusseldorf/

Frankfurt/Main http://frankfurt.usconsulate.gov

Commercial Service

http://export.gov/germany/Contact/Frankfurt/

Hamburg http://hamburg.usconsulate.gov

Leipzig http://leipzig.usconsulate.gov

Munich http://munich.usconsulate.gov

Commercial Service

http://export.gov/germany/Contact/Munich/

Washington-based USG Country Contacts:

U.S. Department of Commerce, International Trade
Administration

http://trade.gov

U.S. Department of State

www.state.gov

USDA - Foreign Agricultural Service, Agricultural Export
Services Division. The website has trade and production
statistics, exporter assistance information, marketing information,
trade policy news and links to the attaché reports.

www.fas.usda.gov

U.S. Department of the Treasury
www.ustreas.gov

Office of the U.S. Trade Representative, Office of Europe and
the Mediterranean
http://www.ustr.gov

G. U.S.-based Multipliers German Missions in the United States
www.germany.info

CMA - German Agricultural Marketing Board, North American
Office
www.germanfoods.org

German American Chamber of Commerce, Inc. (Headquarters)
www.gaccny.com

Representative of German Industry and Trade
www.rgit-usa.com

Agricultural Affairs Office
American Embassy/Berlin
Clayallee 170
14191 Berlin, Germany
Tel: [49][30] 8305-1150
Fax: [49][30] 8431-1935
Email: Agberlin@usda.gov
http://germany.usembassy.gov/fas

The German association of advertising agencies:

Gesamtverband Kommunikationsagenturen e.V.

(German Association of Advertising Agencies)

Friedensstr. 11

60311 Frankfurt a. M.

Telephone: [49][69] 2560080

Telefax: [49][69] 236883

www.gwa.de/

Agricultural Affairs Office

American Embassy/Berlin

Clayallee 170

14191 Berlin, Germany

Tel: [49][30] 8305-1150

Fax: [49][30] 8431-1935

Email: Agberlin@fas.usda.gov

Germany Trade and Invest

The inward investment promotion agency of the Federal

Republic of Germany

Friedrichstraße 60

10117 Berlin, Germany

Telephone: [49][30] 2000 99 0

Telefax: [49][30] 2000 99 111

www.gtai.com

Germany Trade & Invest

1776 I Street, N.W.

Suite 1000

Washington, D.C.

20006

Telephone: 202 629 5711

Telefax: 202 347 7473

www.gtai.com

Germany Trade & Invest

321 Clark Street,

Suite 1425

Chicago, IL 60654

Telephone: 312 377 6131

Telefax: 312 377 6134

www.gtai.com

Germany Trade and Invest

One Embarcadero

Center, Suite 1060

San Francisco, CA 94111

Telephone: 415 248 1246

Telefax: 415 627 9169

www.gtai.com

Germany Trade and Invest

75 Broad Street, 21st Floor

New York, NY 10004

Telephone: 212 584 9715

Telefax: 212 262 6449

www.gtai.com

U.S. Banks and Local Correspondent Banks:

Bank of America

National Association

An der Welle 5

60322 Frankfurt, Germany

Telephone: 49-69-71001-0

Website: www.bankofamerica.com

Citigroup Global Markets Germany

Reuterweg 16

60323 Frankfurt am Main, Germany

Telephone: 49-69-1366 0

Website: www.citi.com

JP Morgan GmbH

Junghofstr. 14

60311 Frankfurt am Main, Germany

Telephone: 49-69-7124 0

Telefax: 49-69-7124 2209

Website: www.jpmorgan.com

Goldman-Sachs & CO

Messeturm

Friedrich-Ebert-Anlage 49

60308 Frankfurt am Main, Germany

Telephone: 49-69-7532 1000

Telefax: 49-69-7532 2800

Website: www.gs.com

Merrill Lynch Bank AG

Main Tower

Neue Mainzer Strasse 52

60311 Frankfurt am Main, Germany

Telephone: 49-69-5899 5000

Telefax: 49-69-5899 4000

Website: www.ml.com

Morgan Stanley AG

Junghofstr. 13-15

60311 Frankfurt am Main, Germany

Tel: 49-69-2166-0

Telefax: 49-69-2166-2099

Website: www.morganstanley.com

The Internationalist

www.internationalist.com

www.ingramcontent.com/pod-product-compliance
Lightning Source LLC
Chambersburg PA
CBHW051328170526
45166CB00002B/720